Praise for *Best Copy Av*

A compulsive descent into da .... of the
invincibility of our fragile hearts. Nicorvo leaves it all on the
page . . . a bravura performance.

—**Junot Díaz**, Pulitzer Prize–winning author of
The Brief Wondrous Life of Oscar Wao

An unflappable, unrelenting examination of abuse and violence,
Best Copy Available holds nothing back. Nicorvo is fearless as he
confronts the past, and fearless as he steps into his future.

—**Ann Hood**, New York Times best-selling author of
Comfort: A Journey through Grief

The (true) story unfolding in *Best Copy Available* is almost unre-
lentingly bleak but that relentlessness also makes it difficult to
put down. The voice is jagged, dangerous, compelling, and, above
all, *appropriate.*

—**Geoff Dyer**, author of
The Last Days of Roger Federer

I have read so many accounts of assault and abuse, and I've never
read a book like this. This is a tenacious telling. There was not a
single sentence I'd read before—*Best Copy Available* is new in its
lack of anticipation, in its headlong pursuit of the experience of
bringing a boy into being inside the man who is finally telling
the abuse. This book is such a valuable addition, and it's patron-
izing to say how proud I am that Nicorvo got this down, that he
wrote the damn book, so I won't say that. But he went back for
the boy, and he took him by the hand. *Best Copy Available* breaks
my heart. Such life.

—**Lacy Crawford**, author of *Notes on a Silencing*

Nicorvo is an incredible talent who deals with almost unthink-
able subjects with enthralling prose, humor, and mysterious
grace. Deeply felt, and darkly funny, *Best Copy Available* is a must-
read memoir that can show the world how to love again in the
shadow of sexual violence.

—**Jen Percy**, author of *Demon Camp*
and *Girls Play Dead*

This book set my heart and mind on fire. Nicorvo is a magician:
he has taken tragedy and transformed it into art.

—**Saïd Sayrafiezadeh**, author of
When Skateboards Will Be Free

This hugely compelling book manages to do many things exceedingly well. It's a propulsive true crime story—fast-paced and pitch perfect—as well as a poetic, meditative reflection that haunts with its hard-won wisdom. It's generous and funny and quirky and, against all odds, affirming. Nicorvo has written an original and important book.

—**Beth Ann Fennelly**, author of
Heating & Cooling: 52 Micro-Memoirs

Nicorvo's memoir is a gut-wrenching exploration of the sexual abuse foisted upon both a mother and son. In his unique narrative voice, Nicorvo shares their intertwined memories and in doing so, raises himself to the light. *Best Copy Available* is an important book for all readers. It will stand solidly on the shelf along with other classic memoirs such as *Educated*, *The Glass Castle*, and *Notes on a Silencing*.

—**Pamela Klinger-Horn**, Valley Bookseller

Painfully elegant yet triumphant, Nicorvo's thoughtful writing explores society and the effects on individuals and families as he faces appalling events in his past. Nicorvo and his demons circle each other warily, sizing each other up like big cats competing for territory, the demon cats doing their best to disrupt Nicorvo's peace of mind, and scare off the writer intent on facing and analyzing these demons out of existence. It's an honor to be allowed to perch on his shoulder and accompany him through this journey he so gracefully relates.

—**Jamie Fiocco**, owner, Flyleaf Books;
recent president of the American Booksellers
Association

You do not have to be a child of the '80s to deeply feel and understand each piece of Nicorvo's story and the glowing truth that beats throughout *Best Copy Available*. Is it possible to be sorry, and angry, and sick, and haunted by a book? Because simple, lucid touchstones are absolutely essential to jarring loose the terror, and also prying open any story itself—if any (one) of us is to have a chance at grace. I somehow placed my feet onto the floor upon closing this book's final page and felt—quite literally—as if I might fall much deeper than to my knees in holy gratitude for the chance and purpose of being alive on this Earth. What a work.

—**Joanna Parzakonis**, co-owner,
this is a bookstore & Bookbug

THE

SUE

WILLIAM

SILVERMAN

BEST COPY

PRIZE

FOR

CREATIVE

NONFICTION

SELECTED BY GEOFF DYER

AVAILABLE

A TRUE CRIME MEMOIR

By Jay Baron Nicorvo

THE
UNIVERSITY
OF
GEORGIA
PRESS
ATHENS

Published by the University of Georgia Press
Athens, Georgia 30602
www.ugapress.org
© 2024 by Jay Baron Nicorvo
All rights reserved
Designed by Kaelin Chappell Broaddus
Set in 9.8/13.5 Joanna Nova Book by Kaelin Chappell Broaddus
Printed and bound by Sheridan Books, Inc.
The paper in this book meets the guidelines for permanence
and durability of the Committee on Production Guidelines for
Book Longevity of the Council on Library Resources.

Most University of Georgia Press titles are available from popular e-book vendors.

Printed in the United States of America
28 27 26 25 24 C 5 4 3 2 1

The Eldridge Cleaver quote is from Eldridge Cleaver,
    Soul on Ice (New York: Random House, 1999).
The first John Berger quote is from John Berger, Ways of Seeing:
    Based on the BBC Television Series (London: Penguin, 1972).
The second John Berger quote is from John Berger, And Our Faces,
    My Heart, Brief as Photos (New York: Knopf Doubleday, 1991.)
The Samuel Beckett quote is from Samuel Beckett, Proust and Three
    Dialogues with Georges Duthuit (Richmond, UK: Calder, 1970).
The Fintan O'Toole quote is from Fintan O'Toole, "Where Lost
    Bodies Roam," New York Review of Books, June 7, 2018.
And the Mamie Till quote is from Christopher Benson and
    Mamie Till-Mobley, Death of Innocence: The Story of the Hate Crime
    That Changed America (New York: Random House, 2011).

Library of Congress Cataloging-in-Publication Data

Names: Nicorvo, Jay Baron, author.
Title: Best copy available : a true crime memoir / by Jay Baron Nicorvo.
Description: Athens : The University of Georgia Press, [2024]
Identifiers: LCCN 2024003603 (print) | LCCN 2024003604 (ebook) |
    ISBN 9780820367361 (paperback) | ISBN 9780820367378 (epub) | I
    SBN 9780820367385 (pdf)
Subjects: LCSH: Nicorvo, Jay Baron. | Authors, American—21st century—
    Biography. | Authors, American—21st century—Family relationships. |
    Sexual abuse victims—Family relationships. | Families—United States.
Classification: LCC PS3614.I3548 Z46 2024 (print) | LCC PS3614.I3548 (ebook) |
    DDC 364.15/32092 [b]—dc23/eng/20240316
LC record available at https://lccn.loc.gov/2024003603
LC ebook record available at https://lccn.loc.gov/2024003604

For Aunt Gail, the very first
to show me art's insistence,
and for you, Mom, because just
like you, I did my damnedest

Author's Note

Out of respect for privacy, especially in the case of certain minors, I have changed names and identifying characteristics of some people represented in these pages.

Also by Jay Baron Nicorvo

Deadbeat: Poems

The Standard Grand: A Novel

Open with Sharon. She's delivering pizzas for Domino's, her night job. This is the Jersey shore in 1984. Specifically, Monmouth County on February 24, just after midnight. A cold rain intermittently falls. Born in the USA, Bruce Springsteen's seventh album, is a few months from its historic release. Even so, the Boss (who prefers Scooter) is every bit the hometown boy made good after the breakout success of the first Born album, 1975's Born to Run.

Sharon's my mom, and Mom's younger sister by a year, Gail, has been seen slow dancing at a bar with Clarence the "Big Man" Clemons, tenor saxophonist of Springsteen's E Street Band. Mid-'80s in and around Asbury Park, a Black man and a white woman in an embrace, even if the brother's famous, is sniffed at, and far worse, but Gail couldn't care less. Gail says people are real assholes.

Gail plays a little sax. She writes her own songs on electric guitar, a Fender Stratocaster she lets me and my two little brothers wail on. We take turns pulling waawaas from the whammy bar. She owns a cozy two-bedroom bungalow on a dead-end street a block from the boardwalk in Long Branch. Like Mom, Gail's a divorcée, though Gail's been at it longer. She has hobbies. She watercolors. She macramés. She owns a Manta Windjammer, a three-wheel landsailer with a bucket seat, that she breaks down and piles into her Wise delivery truck. We eat the out-of-date potato chips on the ride. She pieces the Windjammer back together in an empty parking lot on a blustery day, tucking one of us at a time in her lap. We whip a couple of inches over the asphalt at thirty MPH or more, hooting the whole way. Up on blocks beside her house, she's fixing an old powerboat, a twenty-four-foot inboard. She rechristens it *Gail Warnings*. When we ask why, at age thirty-eight, she has no kids, she says, Please, yous guys are all the kids I can handle.

On the nights Mom works, we're all Gail's.

Covered and gone quiet, Gail's cockatiel perches in its cage. Her cats, Earthstar and Wolfie, hide from us in the closet, under the bed. Splayed out next to the pregnant ferret curled in a furry circle—Maria, named after the wind, and rhymed with fire, sort of, in the best-known song from *Paint Your Wagon*—we three boys sleep sprawled on her sprawling sectional couch.

A leftover from her marriage, the couch doesn't occupy the living room; the couch is the living room.

Drooling into it, my little brothers and I sleep wearing legwarmers Gail fashioned for us, cutting the sleeves off three old sweaters. She took us to the video store. We rented a movie and stayed up late, on this, a Thursday. Dane and I have school tomorrow.

Maybe because we're three boys being raised by two women, we have no care for sports and love watching *Flashdance*, bopping for hours like maniacs, dancing like we've never danced before. When I told Gail it was R-rated, she answered, It's not like it's violence, it's just sex.

A couple hours before sunrise, Gail wakes us in the dark, yanking off our legwarmers. She piles us yawning into her car, not bothering to buckle us in, and drives us the fifteen minutes—there's no traffic at that hour and she runs the red lights—to Fort Monmouth Army Base.

● ● ●

While my brothers and I still sleep on the couch, across a six-mile stretch of town, as Thursday night turns to Friday morning, at about 12:15 a.m., Mom is through the West Gate of the army base for the second time that shift. She parks her car, a jalopy Plymouth Valiant with a cracked windshield. She remembers—all these years later—leaving it running, but that's not what she'll tell the investigator.

Weather data of those early morning hours has the temperature at ten degrees above freezing with a twenty-mile-per-hour wind. Another source—more comprehensive and detailed, more subjective but subtly so—describes those hours: *Cloudy, raining off and on all night, temperature about forty-five degrees, ground wet, dark.*

Soon to turn forty, Mom's a bombshell. Years earlier, a photo of her ran in most Jersey newspapers the weekend of 15 October 1971. In the *Courier-Post* of Camden, Mom sits faintly smiling—somehow not sultry—in a silk robe. Her bangs are smartly chopped. The picture runs under the headline *Playboy Bunnies Hired on the Spot*.

• • •

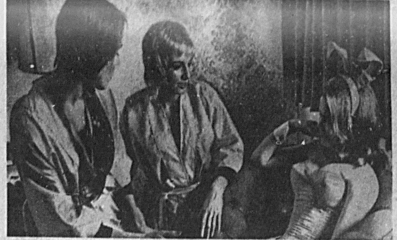

—UPI-Courier-Post Telefax

FINE POINTS of being a Playboy bunny are explained to would-be bunnies Karen Kotoas of Colonia (left) and Sharon Nicorvo of Woodbridge (center), by Leslie Morley, one of the features of a "bunny hunt" conducted yesterday at the new Playboy hotel and resort in McAfee, Sussex County.

・・・

Her mother- and father-in-law were scandalized, and Mom refused the job, which was crappy. Scantily clad cocktail waitress, more demeaned than glorified. Work at the Playboy Club hotel and resort due to open that December. Same job Gloria Steinem accepted a few years earlier, albeit undercover and assuming a false identity, Marie Catherine Ochs, for a two-part exposé that ran in consecutive issues of *Show*, titled "A Bunny's Tale." Besides, Mom had a job, same one she held since right out of high school.

Till I came along twelve years into her marriage, she was an editorial secretary at the *Perth Amboy Evening News*, later the *News Tribune*, working for Kenneth Michael, the editor who became a publisher of the paper. When she interviewed for the position—which, like the Playboy Club job, she was offered on the spot—she had no idea how to type. That's the kind of beautiful she was, is. But that was a lifetime ago, before she had three boys, before her husband, our father, was a fugitive who fled the state, blowing up their marriage. And yet, and still, and all these years later, she attracts all sorts of attention, most of it unwanted.

The qualities that make her the center of the *Courier-Post* newspaper photo—John Dante, assistant to Hugh Hefner, told the reporter, "The criterion is good looks—good looks with a well-proportioned figure"—are the ones that make her a target fifteen years after that photo ran. Doesn't matter that her Domino's uniform, a baggy windbreaker and ball cap, isn't as flattering as a cockeyed pair of bunny ears, a perky cottontail. After what's bound to come, if she were only homelier, fatter—she thinks, forever and again—maybe she would've been left alone, and soon, and for the rest of her life, she'll be overweight.

・・・

As Mom walks to building 1200E, she gets some warm comfort from the pizza box in her arms. This is her seventeenth delivery of the night, and she's in and out in a hurry.

Confronting the wet Atlantic wind—icy, briny—she loathes the rain. Hates the shitty Jersey winters. The bad weather hits her like a cheap vodka martini, dirty, cold but watered down, and boy could she use a drink. Hers is a gimlet, same as her sister's. She can almost taste the Rose's lime juice as she opens the car door of the Valiant—it usually sticks. Apparently, she didn't close it all the way. She slides in, concerned, and that's when the sleeved right forearm shoots under her chin, crushes against her throat, pulls her hard against the seatback.

• • •

CID REPORT OF INVESTIGATION

For use of this form see AR 195-2; the proponent agency is United States Army Criminal Investigation Command

PREPARING AGENCY For: Monmouth Resident Agency First Region, USACIDC Fort Monmouth, NJ 07703-5503	TYPE OF REPORT Final (C)	REPORT NUMBER 0025-84-CID142-75507-6E1C1/ 6P3/ 96-1963
	DATE OF REPORT 26 July 1984	

PLACE OF OCCURRENCE
Parking Lot West of Hemphill Parade Field, Fort Monmouth, NJ 07703

OCCURRENCE		REPORTED	
DATE 24 Feb 84	TIME 0020	DATE 24 Feb 84	TIME 0054
REF SSG (b)(6)(b)(7)(C) MP D/SGT		INVEST SA (b)(6)(b)(7)(C)	

DISTRIBUTION

ACTION COMMANDER	OTHER (Specify)
STAFF JUDGE ADVOCATE	
PROVOST MARSHAL	
CRIME RECORDS CTR	
REGION	
FIELD OFFICE	
FILE	

SIGNATURE OR APPROVING AUTHORITY

(b)(6)(b)(7)(C)

(b)(6)(b)(7)(C)
Special Agent-in-Charge, Ft Monmouth RA
Fort Monmouth, NJ 07703-5503

DETAILS
TITLE:

1. Unknown; Rape and Sodomy   BEST COPY AVAILABLE

VICTIM:

1. NICORVO, Sharon Joan; Civ; 2, Jun 45; Perth Amboy, NJ; F; White; 279 Avenel Blvd, Long Branch, NJ 07740; Rape and Sodomy.

SYNOPSIS: NICORVO delivered a pizza to bldg 1200E, Ft Monmouth, NJ 07703. Upon her return to her vehicle, an unknown black male forced her to drive to the parking lot adjacent to Hemphill Parade Field where he forced her to perform fellatio and then raped her.

This investigation is being terminated prior to the receipt of the Laboratory Report in accordance with CIDR 195-1, par. 3-27 d(8), (9), in that the laboratory report is not relevant to the identification of the perpetrator and there is no apparent potential for solution of this offense. Should the laboratory report provide information of evidentiary value, this investigation will be re-opened and a supplemental report prepared.

EXHIBITS:

A. Attached:

1. Agent's Investigation Report (AIR) of SA (b)(6)(b)(7)(C) 29 Feb 84, in which he details the initial notification of this offense and actions taken during crime scene processing and the preliminary investigation.

2. Rough sketch depicting the crime scene, prepared by SA (b)(6)(b)(7)(C) 24 Feb 84.

WARNING This is a police report, not a legal disposition. The listing of offenses are for crime classification purposes only and are not adjudications of guilt or innocence. Reviewers must analyze the report on that basis and should consult with the supporting Staff Judge Advocate for specific charges. This report is the property of USACIDC the contents of which are not to be distributed outside of your organization without the expressed approval of the Commanding General, USACIDC.

DA FORM 2800   **FOR OFFICIAL USE ONLY**   EDITION OF 1 APR 49, IS OBSOLETE, REPLACES
1 JAN 78   (When Data is Entered)   DA FORM 2800-1, 1 JUN 78, WHICH IS OBSOLETE.

000001

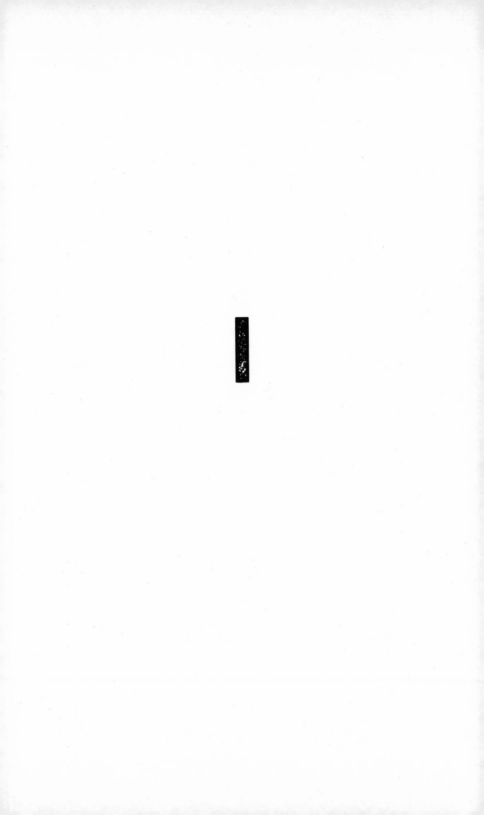

Mama there's wolves in the house
Mama I tried to put them out
And mama I know you're too wise
To wait 'til those wolves make nice

—**Phosphorescent, "Wolves"**

Like the force of gravity, abuse bends space, torques time. The greater the abuse, the greater the gravity. Abuse takes time's arrow and turns it in, on itself. Abuse is the serpent that eats its tail. Abuse works like a wormhole, opening a rent in a moment, any moment. We abused—and aren't we all, at one time or another—are then forever slipping back into that hole, falling toward the unforgettable unfathomable. Stuck in an instant that seems more real than our regular reality. Abuse fucks verb tenses all up and down. Past perfect. Present tense. Future conditional. Abuse demands profanity. Bend it till it breaks. Not just language but thought, too. Abuse is nonlinear. Abuse is repetitive, maddeningly so. Abuse is confusing. Abuse wreaks havoc with pronouns. Abuse ruins chronology. I'm sorry, but much writing about abuse tends to get abuse awfully wrong. Anyone who tries to tell abuse to you straight—linear like—is lying out their fucking ass. That, or trying to sell something. Abuse is autophiliac. Abuse isn't about self-obsession but we abused are stuck—continuously and without pleasure—fucking our fucking selves. You think I enjoy this? You think my mom does? Relaying and reliving this mess? You enjoy this? Get a kick out of it? Sick fuck? Because abuse makes for more feeling and more meaning. Abuse turns the mundane and the coincidental into the monumental, the catastrophic. Abuse is—by nature, by necessity—epic. Abuse is a terribly effective teacher that, redundantly, teaches one single thing. Abuse is how people develop crippling fears of spirals or popes, or decide to take up arms against pizza parlors.

• • •

Christmas Eve on the Jersey Shore, 1981, comes as a shock. The night is clear, starry, and bracing. The dark arrives earlier all the sudden. Below freezing though not Santa kind of weather. No snow. Instead, a cold salt wind whips off the ocean. But this is closer to the climate of Santa than the weather we abandoned. Days before, we lived in Florida. Balmy December highs in the seventies. An airless, months-long escape from the outskirts of Chicago, the IRS zeroing in on us.

Mom and Gail take my two little brothers and me down to the Long Branch boardwalk, closed for winter. A battened-down arcade, the shuttered Haunted Mansion. Mom doesn't care. She's desperate, desperate to get a long look at the ocean. Darker than bedtime. The shushing, whitewater crash of waves.

Mom and Gail grew up tickling the leggy tummies of horseshoe crabs they lifted from Raritan Bay in Sayreville, a run-down Jersey borough flanked by the industrial Amboys, South and Perth. Staten Island just beyond. Long Branch sits some forty-five minutes down the shore. Mom could hardly stand living landlocked for the few years we spent in Illinois—Lake Michigan, by her lights, didn't count for squat—and then the six months we lasted on the lam in Central Florida.

For her, the beach is home. And here in Jersey, the shore-front's filthy. Not as bad as the Syringe Tides of the late '80s but it sure ain't pretty. Not that Dane or I care—more to play with. Shawn's nothing but a wide-eyed bundle, relayed back and forth between Mom and Gail, who's meeting him for the first time.

All along the dark beach, tar balls have washed up, dredged in sand. Even though we don't get near the frigid tide, our hands, and then our winter coats, are quickly tar-covered.

Dane and I play tar babies, just like Br'er Rabbit. We make

our way back to Mom, Gail, and Shawn, and I present what I think is a popped balloon, tarred and sanded.

Yous guys are a mess, Mom says. Oh, Jesus, Jay, put that down for Christ sake.

Maybe it was a party, I tell her. They're all over.

When Dane, nearly three, tries to blow one up, Mom slaps it to the sand, about fumbling Shawn.

Okay, Gail says, time to go.

We're out late. Up way past usual. Mom wanted to attend the early Christmas Eve Mass, but Gail talked her out of it.

You don't have a tree, Shest. No decorations. No presents. Let's take the boys to Midnight Mass at St. Michael's. It's festive. It's free. They can fall asleep. Tomorrow first thing, you bring 'em over to my house. Might even have a little something for each of 'em under the tree.

That rinkydink thing, Mom says, you call that a tree? At's a shrub.

Gail shrugs, a twinkle in her hazel eye, and Gail, starlet beautiful but brassy as a pipe fitting, doesn't often twinkle. It's Christmastime though, so what the hell. Twinkle away.

We drive around looking at strands of light on houses, listening to carols on the car radio. Lots of Sinatra. It's no "Jingle Bells" Christmas Eve in Jersey, not this year. Not for us. Mom's given us fair warning—Santa Claus ain't comin' to town. No, no, no.

This is our blue Christmas. In my memory, I can hear some singer—not Elvis, unless it's the fat, drug-addled Elvis— maybe some croaker blinded by lye. Or one of the Lightnings or the Mamas, come up North, riding the freedom wave of the Great Migration. Dark-ass night, cold-ass ground.

Hark, hear the homemade slide guitar. Played not with the usual broken bottleneck. Oh hell no. These strings are pressed instead with the flat blade of a jackknife. I'm talking true blue Christmas music. Music fit for a refugee newborn-to-be, on the run from Herod, fatherless, carried to term by a young mother, homeless, half out her head with not knowing how in tarnation she got knocked the fuck up in the first place. Baby about to be caught, before hitting the hay, by a middle-aged mensch of a stepfather, a Jew baby birthed in a lean-to—or a cave, by some accounts—as cud-chewing livestock, kosher, look on. Bah. Moo. Baby born—with a birthdate nowhere near the winter solstice—only to be murdered thirty-three years hence in the most painful, public way conceivable at the time. Martyred then mythologized. Stepson of a manual laborer become a god. How's that for upward mobility.

Thinking specifically now about the most American of anthems, "Dark Was the Night, Cold Was the Ground," picked by Carl Sagan to represent all of humanity to the aliens in outer space, on duplicate copies of the Golden Record blasted in opposite directions, for the Voyager missions. If Johnny B. Goode could play a guitar just like a-ringin' a bell, according to Chuck Berry, well then Blind Willie Johnson plays a guitar like wringing the neck of a prize rooster, Goddammit. Lovingly plucking the beautiful bird's feathers. All while humming, maybe moaning, sad, off-key, and awful hungry.

Hard for me to hear that Blind Willie Johnson tune, whatever my intents, and not think—Ah, fuck, in the scene of the rape of America, this here's the soundtrack.

What we're really hearing—in that blind voice, the blind strumming and chord bending—is the sound—if we had the ears to hear—a hollowed-out lynching tree might produce, as men decorate its boughs with the strange fruit of other men, only darker. A ripe giving season of grief. Burdened branches. Maybe, high up, a growth of American mistletoe, parasitic. Pearly white berries, toxic. Dark was the night, cold was the ground alright. And wet. A woe-filled season that often followed fast on the heels of a rape accusation.

Because in that folksy wordlessness, you can almost make out the early, dumbed-down story of antebellum race relations in America, the simplified version anyway: Black man rapes white woman, white man hangs Black man, white man returns home to rape the help. Or his wife, depending. Welcome to Rapeland.

. But I digress. But this is hard. But you must be patient, mustn't you? You're at my mercy. Or am I at yours? I'm begging you now. Working my way round—reluctantly, resentfully—on my knees, to what needs work. Doing the best I'm able, as a certifiable hemmer and hawer. Because today we have stats, provided by the FBI, that say only 8 percent of all sexual abuse claims are fiction, rather than fact. And while there're no real numbers, and no way of ever securing any, it wouldn't be a far cry to assume some inversion of those statistics in the Jim Crow South and before, during Blind Willie Johnson's time, where even the intimation of sexual assault was the quickest surefire way to gather up a hot posse.

But this is Christmas in Jersey, early 1980s, and no one in this story's getting raped or molested. Not just yet. So hold your reindeer. Keep your fucking knickers on.

• • •

Here's how I resee that Yuletide scene—from my troubled perch nearly four decades after the fact—at the tail end of 1981. A poorboy's poor imitation of a Ghost of Christmas Past.

Dropping in—unguided, unhinged—on Mom and Gail, on my two brothers and young me, I see the pair of sisters getting tipsy at Gail's before our nighttime trip to the beach, then church. One gimlet then another. The drive around Long Branch is a swervy adventure. I'm not old enough yet—and the world isn't yet wise enough—to be worried.

Along the way, with Gail behind the wheel, Shawn gets breastfed. When he passes out midsuckle, sweet milk dribbling down his chin, Mom says, Oops, might've gone and spiked the eggnog.

There are no seatbelts never mind car seats. Dane and I tumble round the back, occupy ourselves with our tar-blackened fingers between shoving matches. I stick my sticky finger an inch from his cheek, saying, I'm not touching you, but when we take a turn too wide, I do.

Mom, Dane says. Jay's touching me.

Up front, headed now for St. Michael's on Ocean Avenue, the two middle-aged sisters, newly reunited, are on a gimlet-eyed riff. They're best of friends, these Irish twins, born eighteen months apart. Always have been. Their respective husbands came between them, but no more. Gone are the men and for good, mostly. The three boys here in the charge of these two women will be raised matriarchal for the foreseeable future.

One of the sisters says—and who the hell really knows; it's often hard to tell them apart—Santa's been detained. No, Rudolf caught a sinus cold. Or Donner came down with hoof-and-mouth. I thought it was Donder, Gail says. Or maybe it's Mom. Fine, Mom says, Donder it is. Gail says, Donner's a goner. And Vixen sprained a horn. Gail says this is starting to sound like a song. A jingle. Kinky. No it decidedly is not, Mom says. Not everything's a song, Gail. Top it all off, Santa's little workers went on strike. And Mrs. Claus is having an affair with Kris Kringle. Gail! What. Old King Cole was a merry old soul—King Cole has zilch to do with Christmas. Then who in hell's the Christmas king? At's good King Wencelas. Ain't it Wenceslas? How the hell should I know. Soon they're both wassailing something about the Feast of Stephen.

Dane and I shrug at each other, and I say I'm hungry.

The song peters out. They can't recall the words. I ask for the hundred-zillionth time why's it we get no presents this year.

We've just moved, Mom says. Again. Your present's a roof over your head. Be grateful. Besides, Santa hasn't updated his address book. Too busy making his list, checking it twice.

I press, demanding to know how Santa can tell we've been naughty if he can't even know where we moved.

Gail says not to worry. Have faith in Santa.

When I ask if Santa's God, Mom says, Once we get all settled, Santa'll make it up to yous—if yous're good. Satan never disappoints good boys. But God on the other hand? The sisters laugh. Mom says sometimes Santa shows—shit, did I just say Satan a second ago?

Yes you did!

I meant Santa not Satan!

Jesus, Gail says, let's get you to church fast.

Mom says, Sometimes *Santa* shows up a few weeks late.

Satan too, Gail says. Then she's singing, So have some sympathy. Some courtesy. And some taste. They laugh, Gail more than Mom. Their laughter's not mean, it's just drunk. But it's Christmas. Have some faith.

• • •

Truth is, Mom's dirt-broke. Barely has money to buy milk and eggs, a loaf of off-brand white bread and some bologna for frying, never mind toys. Gail's given Mom all she could afford, and some more she couldn't, to pay the deposit on half a rental duplex two blocks from the Long Branch Sewerage Authority. The deposit goes to a Wendy Wen, who lives alone in the other half and owns the whole thing. Ms. Wen, no older than Mom, is our neighbor and our landlady, and she speaks better English than we do, with less of an accent, which is maybe why we were renting from her.

This, after our Florida warm spell that lasted half the year: see me and Dane dressed in nothing but our superhero Underoos outside of Kissimmee, while our father, Tony, dodges the taxman by bass fishing. Miles away, he lives in a camper parked on some forty-two acres of swampland he bought with cash. We don't know where, exactly. He's not telling, so Mom won't have to lie to the IRS investigators who come around, sweating in suits, asking insistent questions, wanting to know whereabouts.

Tony stops in for a few minutes every couple days, gives Mom some of the cash he spent years secreting away, brings me a snapping turtle the size of a manhole cover he deposits in our fenced-in backyard. The turtle has a head big as a pail and it looks furious.

Tony, already a stranger, tells me be careful. Turtle has a mean beak. Take off a toe or ten.

Terrified, I go in search of the turtle. How long have I been at this—gone looking for the thing I most fear? All I find is a hole. Burrowed under the fence. Wide enough for me to crawl through. But I'm no Alice. I don't dive in. Not yet.

• • •

Mom lasts six months as the wife of a working-class out-law wanted for a rich man's crime. Tax fraud. Couple weeks before the holidays, she tells Tony she wants a divorce. She wants the boys. Wants to spend Christmas with her sister. She wants enough money to move us to Jersey to be near Gail. Tony doesn't fight, not at first. He tells her not to tell his parents, strict Roman Catholics, who live in Asbury Park. Let him break the damning news. He's resigned, and Mom doesn't have much packing to do. Most everything's still in boxes.

• • •

The Christmas Eve Midnight Mass at St. Michael's promises to be astounding and then stultifying. A Catholic pageant down the center aisle. Robes lined with gold, gold scepters, gold knockoff grail. There are songs, there's chanting. Baskets at the end of poles that parishioners drop cash money into, proudly, but not us. We drop in pocket change. There's Latin, and Gail tells us there's about to be an honest-to-God miracle. See if you can spot it.

Turns out, the miracle is supposed to be some bread turns to Jesus. But when the priest holds over his head a wafer-thin circle he breaks in half, and the so-called bread doesn't turn into a baby, I get bored. Don't even look like bread, I mumble. Then louder, At's not bread, at's a Ritz cracker.

We'd never been steady churchgoers. Before we were born, Mom, raised Irish Catholic, dabbled in Wicca, and Tony, Roman Catholic, hung on their living room wall a black velvet portrait of the devil. For fun. But we three boys were baptized into the Catholic church, just to be safe.

The faithful are called to take Communion. Neither Mom nor Gail gets out of our pew, which draws some frowns, sidelong looks. This I gather, even then, is a shame. It makes me tired. I yawn, and Dane yawns, copying me.

To keep myself awake, I tease him. Poke him, tickle him. I make him yawn again with the power of my yawn. When we're separated—Gail moving between us as Mom breastfeeds Shawn right there in the great big old house of God—we pull faces at each other till we start giggling. And soon we can't stop. Even though nothing's that funny.

An older couple next to us isn't happy. Bah humbug. The old husband, smoky, is watching Mom nurse Shawn, and the old wife, heated, watching her husband, is making a to-do without saying anything. Huffing and tsking. She's a steam engine getting up a full head. Woo-woo.

Gail turns to her fiercely and hisses, What, ain't you never seen the *Madonna and Child*? It's da Vinci and it's Christmas. Grow up. Old hag. And then Gail's shushing us, and each time she shushes, we laugh. When Gail starts laughing, we're goners.

Nothing delights us more than seeing an adult lose it, laughing while trying to scold. We can't control ourselves, Gail can't control us, and then Mom's laughing while Shawn smacks and suckles away—I'm still hungry—slurping and pawing at her great big old breast, her areola golden brown. Size and color of the silver-dollar pancakes she sometimes makes for Dane and me during Saturday-morning cartoons.

Welcome to motherhood, Mom says laughing. See what you been missing? We're all laughing now just 'cause we're all

laughing, and some of us are little kids, and reasonably cute—
Dane's adorable, part dark Irish, part green-eyed Italian—so
the people around us start laughing. Even the old couple upset at Mom for flashing her great big old overflowing tit in
the house of God. I mean it's fucking Christmas Eve, after all,
and then it's over, the laughing fit not the Mass, which lasts
for fucking ever—a part of it, purgatorial, still ongoing—and
our stomachs are sore from so many belly laughs. Before you
know it, we're nodding off. All three of us. We're asleep and
snoring. The adults around us continue to chuckle some, to
themselves, to their God, assuming they know what's good for
them.

● ● ●

Stop being such a bitch, Shest. You Scrooge. Where's your Christmas spirit. You're the one who loves Christmas. I couldn't care
less. You've seen my tree.

Christmas spirit's packed away. In some box. Next to all
Mom's old ornaments.

You still have those?

Course I still have those. Ones the boys haven't broke yet.

We're in the driveway of our new home. It's not a home. It
isn't new. I'm up now and grouchy. My first waking thought—
no presents. I'm about to cry.

Gail's lifting Dane, still asleep, out of the back seat, nudg-
ing me from the car and into our end of the confusing half-a-
house that is a duplex, whatever that's supposed to be.

Inside, when Gail steers me toward the living room, Mom
says, Where you taking him. Bedroom's this way.

I say, What's that smell?

I know where the bedroom is, Gail says, covering my
mouth with her hand. I picked the place out. I paid for it, remember.

I pull away her hand, say, Smells like the woods.

Shush, Gail says.

Cardboard boxes line the hallway, cardboard in the kitchen, boxes in the dining room, under and on the massive Paul Bunyan dining room table.

Gail guides me around the corner, and I start screaming and yelling. Dane wakes up kicking and punching. Gail's smiling and shushing. And Mom shouts, What! What in hell—what's wrong?

Santa came! I yell, Santa! Santa! He came! He came!

When Shawn wakes up wailing, Mom says, Great, you woke the Goddamn baby.

The living room has been cleared of everything but the wine-dark sectional couch and a big, bright Christmas tree. The pine smell brings inside the out-of-doors. Colored lights. Tinsel in the branches. An angel on top. Gold and red garlands. The ornaments are simple Styrofoam balls covered in fine nylon thread, red, yellow, blue. And presents. Loads of presents.

Mom's turn to twinkle now. And cry. Oh, Gail, she says. You did all this? But, wha—how?

Not me, Gail says. Santa. She shrugs. Merry Christmas, Shest.

A minute later, she says, All the gifts, they came care of Santa's helpers. Pat and Joe, Tuna and Clark. Bob Madebach. Ernie. Others. My friends. Yours. Ours. Someone must've let 'em know you might be short this year. So. Gail gives me a nudge. Now yous can't unwrap them till tomorrow morning. But you can each open one now. Right, Shest? Jay, why don't you go find one for each of yous. Go on.

• • •

Mom tucks me in, smiling, on a mattress on the floor, saying, First thing we do is get you and Dane some bunk beds. How's that sound?

Dane's asleep on a mattress next to mine. Can I get the top?

Sure.

You're sad?

I'm not sad. Mom laughs. I'm just so happy I can't help keep from crying.

I wipe her tears. There.

Thank you. She kisses me. It's all going to be okay. Okay? I promise you, Jay.

We got presents, I say and yawn. I got a watch. It's a calculator.

Yes, you got presents. You must've been good.

I think.

Yes, I think, too. And if you be good, keep being a good little man of the house like you've been, Santa'll always come. Even when you least expect it. She kisses me again, tells me merry Christmas and, before she's even out the door, it's Christmas morning. I wake Dane, telling him get up. Get up. It's Christmas! Know what Christmas is?

He blinks. Rubs his eyes, shrugs. Snaps awake, says, Lights. And presents. Come on.

Our first Christmas back in Jersey turns out to be a bonanza. Baby toys for Shawn, a little car dashboard with a steering wheel and gearshift. A key that clicks when you turn the ignition. A Fisher-Price Play Family Farm, its red barn and silo. When you open the barn doors, the barn moos. Not like a cow moos. The barn moos like a duck getting stepped on. Dane and I get a Lite-Brite. Fishing poles. A Flexible Flyer sled. Can we? Can we? A CHiPs Hot Cycle Big Wheel. A Speak & Spell. Hungry Hungry Hippos. Perfection. A Tyco Firebird 300 Slot Set with nightglow guardrails around the turns, and two Pontiac Firebird Trans Ams with working headlights. There are *Empire Strikes Back* action figures, some we already have—Lando Calrissian, Bossk, Han Solo—but we don't care. It's the best Christmas ever because it promised to be the worst and wasn't.

When Mom asks if we got everything we wanted, I say yes. Every single thing.

Dane shrugs, shakes his head no.

No? Mom jumps up and tickles him till he squeals. When she stops tickling, he tells her don't.

Don't tickle?

He shakes his head. No.

Okay, no more tickling.

No, don't stop.

She tickles him till he begs her to stop. What else, she says, what else could you possibly've wanted?

Dane catches his breath, still smiling from all the tickling. He says, A doll.

• • •

Mom says it doesn't happen like that, our Christmas of 1981. She has some recollection of wrapping presents in the basement of the duplex while we play upstairs.

She says, And do you remember when Tony showed up?

No. Not at all.

Drove up all the way from Florida with Uncle Paul. Showed up on Christmas Day, unannounced. Tony and Paul in their matching toupees. And they didn't come with presents. They came with cash and they didn't stay long.

I have no memory of that, I tell her. I tell her that, in her story of that day, retold to us over the years, she's as surprised as we are by the gifts from all Gail's friends.

Yea, she says. You might be right. Your memory for these things is better than mine.

I don't know that's true. What I do know is that when I remember something like that Christmas, and decide to write it, my memory is kicked up like a hive. I recall more detail than I can at any another time in my waking life. Writing focuses recall. Disciplines the mind. Trains it to see and hear things, things that aren't actually there. I can't always trust those details, or the dialogue, especially. At times, I have clear memories of specific lines that were spoken, even though it's not possible.

Problem is, once I write a memory down, the written version overwrites my memory. Like reading a good book, one you live with and return to for years to reread. Only then, a movie version comes out and you make the mistake of seeing it. From that moment on, and for the rest of your life, you can't unsee the movie. The actors are the characters in your mind forevermore.

In that way, writing is memory, and a book becomes a mind.

• • •

We're at a grocery store, and it has a toy aisle. I harangue Mom till she tells Dane and me we can each pick out one toy. So long as it isn't expensive. I don't remember what I choose. Dane picks out a doll.

Mom asks, You sure you want a doll?

He nods, grave.

The doll is like a Barbie, busty and blond, but not a Barbie. It's a Jordache fashion doll. It wears jeans like Mom's wearing. Shoulder-length hair like Mom. Mom's blue eyes. Even I notice the doll is a tiny Mom. She looks at me to see if I care. I shrug. And she says, Okay. You want a doll, you got a doll. And for a few days, she's flattered.

• • •

Dane's being a brat. He's pulling the cat's tail. He's harrumphing around like a hungry toad. Maybe he's tired. Maybe this is before Mom figures out that the least little bit of caffeine, in the smallest taste of chocolate, gets him ornery and angry. He pushes me for no reason, or no reason I can recall. When I tell Mom, he's sent to his room, which is our room.

Ten minutes later, when Mom goes in to see if he's ready to come out and behave, she finds him sitting cross-legged, facing the corner, tucked beyond the dresser. He's banging something against the linoleum floor. He has his blond Jordache doll bent over his knee. He's spanking her, saying. Bad. Bad. Better behave. Or be bad. Bad.

• • •

Dodge taxes. Ditch sons. Assault mothers. Molest kids. Knife grandfathers. This what it means to be a man in America? This isn't the soft power of those more in control. This is its opposite, what the powerless are left with: hard weakness. These American men aren't hollow. These are men full of holes. Holes bored into them by other, more powerful men. The weak men then drill holes in the women, the kids, found within arm's reach, feeling a perverse hunger to fill other people full of holes. Or fill their holes. That's what I witness anyway—though I don't know it then—as we cling from a bottom rung of the American socioeconomic ladder, and during my most formative years. Time to climb? But the ladder's rungs are made from the bones of women and kids.

• • •

My brothers and I are snuggled on the sectional couch at home. Mom's at work, and I don't know why we're not at Gail's but we're not. It's a Monday, 28 February 1983.

Our sitters this night have never sat for us before. Uncle Donald and Aunt Carol—and maybe our teenage cousins Bridget and Brian—are over and they let us stay up past our bedtimes. Something monumental is about to occur.

We like Aunt Carol, but we love Uncle Donald.

Uncle Donald's a man, and not just any man. He's a fireman. He's a father, and we're boys, fatherless. A former member of the 101st Airborne and a Vietnam vet, he's sweet as can be. On a volunteer basis, he drives the back end of the biggest firetruck in the history of firetrucks, for the Red Bank Fire Department, the hook-and-ladder. It's so long it's got two cabs, steering wheels in front and back, and our Uncle Donald drives the back.

We go see his softball games against the police. Uncle Donald isn't really our uncle, but calling him what he is—First Cousin, Once Removed Donald—doesn't make sense. Donald's mom and Mom's mom were sisters, and, like us, Uncle Donald grew up fatherless.

We watch *The Benny Hill Show*, like we do every weekday evening, and we run around like mad while "Yakety Sax" plays during the closing credit roll, always racy and sped up, as Benny gets happily pursued by bosomy women, and often bopped smack in the kisser with something or other.

Then, things turn serious on the couch. I'm confused. The fun ends abruptly. We're told to behave, to be quiet, to settle in and shut it.

On the couch, we are five Americans, and we are doing exactly the same thing at exactly the same time as 106 million other Americans. We're all tuned in together to CBS to watch the final episode of M*A*S*H.

Before I fall asleep, I look up to see Uncle Donald. My eyes light on the tattoo inked bluish on his forearm, the Airborne badge, a parachute with wings, and then I see he's crying. I want to tell him it's going to be okay but I don't. I just close my eyes and sleep curled in his tattooed arm.

● ● ●

Gail herds my little brothers and me into the lobby of Patterson Army Community Hospital. We're cranky and groggy. We fell back asleep in the car but we're awake now, confused and tired. It's too early for school.

Here we are again, in 1984. February 24, some time after midnight. Ground wet, dark. Hard to know if we've gone back or jumped ahead. Maybe neither. Maybe we're always here.

Walking, disoriented, more like a drunk than a toddler, Shawn's unconscious on his feet. I know a drunk when I see one. Weekends are filled with them, always Gail and Mom, but weekdays are dry. This means there're fewer tears on weekdays but also less laughs. Weeknights feel safer and lacking in fun.

Gail lifts and carries Shawn, and I'm jealous.

Shawn's towheaded and blue-eyed. He's cupcake cute and sweet, and women are endlessly trying to gobble him up. As the oldest, I'm painfully aware that, at age seven, I'm washed up. My adorable days are long behind me. My blond hair's going dun brown, and I'm the only one of us with brown eyes. Told I look like our Italian father, I have little idea what our father looks like. No understanding of what it means to be half Italian. Shawn looks like Mom, an Irish angel, radiant. I want to kick him.

The florescent hospital lights blare and flicker in the drop ceiling.

I round a corner ahead of Dane.

Sitting there, worrisome, hunkers a blond woman, ugly. Or I think it's a woman. She looks like the boxers I've seen on TV, the losers. Rocky Balboa after his first bout with Clubber Lang. She reaches out a bandaged hand. I half-expect her to yell, *Yo, Adrian!* Instead, she says my name.

I don't know her, not really. I shy away as she pulls me close. I look to Gail, who nods, teary, and Gail's no crier. Gail's the tough sister, cynical where Mom's sentimental.

This seated woman, her face is seriously fucked. Both eyes bruised blue, one swollen nearly shut, busted lip, fat. Bridge of her nose split and bandaged with what I know is a butter-fly. I've had a few gashes—on my forehead, the corner of my eye—butterflied. She's crying, this woman, hugging me hard, and it's her voice I find familiar, a little croaky, caved in and small. I recognize her Jersey shore smell, briny hairspray and Giorgio, that loud perfume, blinding, like a rose screaming in rubbing alcohol. Her hug though—its warmth and welcome discomfort—I know as home.

Mom? I push away from her, making room to touch her puffy eye. Jesus, does it hurt?

Mom? Dane's not asking her a question; Mom has become a question. He takes a step back, out of reach. Dane's stern and distrustful. In his infancy, the only time he complained was when held. Here as a five-year-old, he doesn't mind being handled so much anymore, but you can't look at him long. And for some reason, if woken up, he comes to consciousness kicking and punching.

At this point in our lives, Dane's the smart son, moody and brooding. He'll grow up to be the handsome one. A cracked-but-not-broken heartbreaker, the most devastating kind. Undereducated and, as a result, too smart for his own damn good. Dark-haired, green-eyed, Dane's not black Irish, not northern Italian. Dane's American. We all are, in our own mixed-up way. We're mutty—this is our resilience—and no one gets Dane—not then, not now—no one but me. And even though Dane's the smart one, I'm no fucking dull tool. Since I was three, when asked what I want to be when I grow up, I've been answering, Aeronautical engineer.

Most people we meet don't know what that is. I don't either, though I can say it as if I mean it. Then Mom interrupts, Tony taught you that. When I ask who Tony is, Mom says something like, Your father. Who always wanted to be an airline pilot. For that, you need a college degree. But the jerk got himself expelled for stealing electronics from the school. And 'cause he's not a college student anymore, he goes and gets drafted into Vietnam. Now somehow—don't ask me how—he managed to convince the army he was out of his mind. Was able to control his heart by concentrating. Spent six months on a military psych ward and got a medical discharge. Found a job as a glorified ditchdigger, installing in-ground pools. Moved us outside Chicago so he could dig his own holes instead of dig holes for his boss. Did that the six months of the year the ground wasn't frozen stiff. Rest of the time your father would hang glide. We's would drive hours to find an Illinois hill. Nothing but open sky for miles. Way off in the distance—teeny, tiny—maybe one single little itsy-bitsy tree.

He'd get his running start, your father would, hang glider all harnessed over him, take off, and before you knew it he would fly straight into that sad little tree. Tony was the Charlie Brown of hang gliders. Then your brothers came along. And your father, apparently, did all this while not paying taxes— unbeknownst to me—because it was the end of the 1970s. Screw Nixon was his thinking I guess. The asshole. Your father, not Nixon. Though Nixon was also an asshole. 'Scuse my language. And here we are. Aeronautical engineer, for heaven sake.

• • •

We're a couple years from seeing the horror show of Tobe Hooper's *Invaders from Mars* remake, where adult bodies are colonized by Martians, the grotesque skin tabs on their disgusting adult necks turning to tiny horns, but the wordless idea—that just beneath the surface, parents are alien creatures determined to do harm—squirms in us at all times. Still, I can tell that Dane, too, isn't sure that this woman in the army hospital lobby is Mom. She's like a purple-paper carbon of Mom, or worse.

From Gail's arms, Shawn says, Me to kiss it, Mommy?

Somehow Shawn—more simply and quickly—has figured out that this is our mom, she's hurt, and she could use our help.

Shit, I say.

Jay, Gail says, quit all your Goddamn swearing. He's not getting this from me, Shest. Was it that *Flashdance* movie? Where's this coming from? Jesus, Jay. And stop saying Jesus!

You just did.

But yous go to Catholic school for Christsakes. Sorry, Shest. This is Gail's nickname for Mom, a sort of shortening of sio-stra, Polish for "sister," but none of us are Poles, we all have Jersey accents, and we sound like foulmouthed douchebags even at the gentlest of times, like this one, so Shest comes out of Gail's mouth like she's slurring the word chest at my mom, who's busty to begin with. It's all a little indecent. And very Jersey.

Mom's sobbing, and laughing some. She's the easy crier, the easy laugher, but there's nothing easy about this. Her crying hurts her. Tonight it hurts us all. It's okay, Mom says, laugh crying. It'll be okay.

Christ, Shest, Gail says. Let's get you home.

No. Mom's angry. Back to your house.

Yeah, sure, whatever. Let's just get the boys outta here and go. Where's your car?

But what the hell, Mom? I say. What's going on?

Mom looks at Gail for a long moment—What? I say—then Mom looks at me.

She swallows, wipes her eyes, and Dane helps her, kissing up now after denying her earlier.

I seem to have an inability to act cute anymore. I've got sarcasm covered, can do snide without even trying, and our sneaky substitute babysitter, Richie, is teaching me all the curse words in the book. Even some of the curses kept out of the book because they're too ass-fucking filthy. But if I tell Mom or Gail, I am dead. Richie will absolutely fucking kill me, he swears on his cunty mother, who lives across the street from Gail.

Mom presses her lips so tightly together that the split top lip weeps a little, not blood. Looks like a droplet of Orange Crush. The tip of her tongue finds it. She can't meet my eye. She's putting on her best face. She says, Jay, I got mugged.

• • •

Put that way, the assault doesn't sound so terrible. The mugging doesn't sound very believable either. We're kids but that doesn't make us idiots. Adults are so stupid to think children are simple. I look at Dane. He too seems unsatisfied with this mugging explanation—sounds like she was hit in the fucking face with a coffee cup—and when I look too long at Dane, he says, Stop looking at me. When I don't look away, he says, Mom, Jay won't stop looking at me.

Jesus, I say, looking down, and then we're ready to go.

Shawn's fallen asleep in Gail's arms, chubby cheek pressed against her shoulder.

I have to admit, he is pretty cocksucking cute.

Dane and I each take one of Mom's hands. We help her to stand, smashed-up face and all. We three keep holding hands on the way out, until Dane, pulling five-year-old free, says, I don't *want* the dumb hand with the dumb mummy thumb.

● ● ●

I doubt Dane spoke those very words but I wouldn't put it past him. He said stuff like that all the time.

My son at five years old, like Dane, has a way with language, and at that age Dane was reticent but bright. When he said something, you snapped to and stared at him, blinking. His observations were keen or cutting, and he could be mean. We all could, all of us save Shawn, who does try. He's just too damn cute to be taken seriously.

● ● ●

I've been obsessed with this night ever since that night. My obsession has gone on so long that most of the reasons are lost to me.

Mom was lying, and I knew it. That was probably reason number one. A mugging. Bullshit. Mom didn't lie, hardly ever. It amazes me the way a lie works, how like trauma, how like gravity, it distorts space, warps time. Those who live with the distortion can't help but feel, at the deepest level of awareness, a compulsion to know, if not alter, the distortion, while likewise wanting nothing to do with it, finding it repulsive.

It wasn't till I was an adult that I understood how much her lie in that moment protected me, how her deception of my brothers and me—though me mostly, because I was the only one who would remember—saved me. Her small distortion prevented a far greater warping. The good lie. The best possible light.

But back then, and for years, for my entire childhood, I resented that lie. I held it against her, even hated her at times for telling it.

Part of my fixation on that night was born out of her lie. There was a mystery there. Some secret. A story for adults only. One they didn't think I was capable of understanding. But we were kids allowed to see R-rated movies, and as a kid, I was an instigator. I pitted myself against my brothers or my brothers against each other. I liked to get a rise out of an adult, any adult. Seeing some grown-up change, getting him to respond, even if the response was anger, felt affirming. I wanted adults to acknowledge me, to know I was there. I wanted to know the adults in my life were around, that they wouldn't up and leave at some sign of trouble I hadn't been told about, because I was too young, and I'd never see that adult again.

• • •

Alone, I cross the street, to Richie's house. Richie isn't home. It's just his mom, Jessica, chain-smoking, her straight hair down to her heinie. I mean her ass. She wears a bandanna, and she reminds me of a singer Gail listens to sometimes, a man, Willie Nelson, who makes me think of Kermit the Frog.

Jessica invites me in, off the front porch, says they're watching a scary movie. Her boyfriend's lanky, a scraggly beard, sunken cheeks. He might be starving. Drinking a can of beer, he keeps saying to the TV, That boy's smart as a fucking whip.

The bungalow is identical to Gail's but reversed, not by layout as much as by aura. Dark where Gail's is light. Shadowy where Gail's glints with stained glass and runs wild with pets and my brothers and me. If this bungalow is smoke, Gail's is fur. Richie's house is a negative of Gail's, and I don't know why I'm by myself with his mom and her boyfriend, in that tight smoke-filled room, and maybe I'm not. Maybe I'm mis-remembering. Maybe I'm dreaming or making it the fuck up. But I don't think so. The thing about memory is, for most of us most of the time, it's what we have, and one theory of mind holds that our memories are analog. Recalling involves over-writing. A memory is a copy of a copy. The more often we re-call a real time and place, the further we get from the real.

Because I remember—both at gut level and in the back of my mind—growing upset there in Richie's mom's house. A wet knot gathers in my throat, choking me. My stomach makes and unmakes a fist. At this age, six or seven or so, I've figured out what this throat knot means for me, what comes next—I'm about to break into tears—but I don't know how to keep it from happening. I don't know where Mom is, why Gail's not here.

The secondhand smoke fills the living room like floodwa-ter. I want to surface, to breathe, but can't. I'm drowning un-der what will soon be the burn of my crying. The shades have been drawn for the movie. And she's nice, Jessica, I like her, but I'm scared. Her boyfriend is saying again, Lord, that boy's smart as a Goddamn whip.

The boy looks like me—bowl haircut, big brown eyes, lost —and I want to be smart as he is, whip-smart. He's running through a hedge maze in snow. He's retracing his tracks. Walking backward, placing, carefully but quickly, precisely, each foot into the previous snowy impression of his foot, like his life depends on it.

A man chases the whip-smart boy with an ax, and I'm told the man is the boy's dad.

• • •

I sneak into Mom's room. She's out, I don't know where. I look under her bed for a stack of magazines I'm told she keeps there, but there's nothing but dust bunnies. I open the drawers of her dresser. It's massive. Paul Bunyan furniture she calls it. She moved it out of the Illinois house before the taxmen auctioned off all our possessions and sold the house out from over us. The furniture's far too big for our thousand-square-foot duplex. Mom's bedroom is the bed. Its ceiling-scraper headboard. The bed's so big you have to edge along the walls to move in and out of the room. The headboard has two columns on either side. An overhang I can stand under. It's got lights that shine down from above, but the lights don't work. The dresser, too, is humongous. I open one drawer, the bottom. It takes all my strength. Inside are Mom's pantyhose. I don't understand how her legs fit inside. I try to see Mom in the same positions as the women in the magazines Richie shows me. The pantyhose have a white triangle between the deflated legs. I press it to my nose, smell it, and feel my penis come alive. I take off my pants, my undies. I have what I've learned is called a boner. I pull on my mom's pantyhose. The feel of the nylon, tight against my legs, my crotch, is thrilling, and terrifying. I pull them off, shove them back in, closing the drawer on my finger. I cry and fight back my tears, sucking my finger as the blood blisters at my fingertip.

Later, when Mom asks how I did that, I shrug. When she asks if it hurts, I nod.

Throbbing sort of?

I nod.

She goes away, comes back, and asks to see my finger. You trust me?

I nod.

She holds my finger out of sight.

I feel a prick, yell, Ow, and she says, All done.

A drop of blood oozes from the pinprick. That relieves the pressure, she says. Your Poppop, my father, was always smashing his fingers. He worked as a mason. A bricklayer. He built our house when I was your age. Gail and me troweled on the mortar and Poppop set the bricks. When he got blood blisters under his fingernails, he'd take his drill and drill a hole straight through the nail.

• • •

In Gail's front windows dangle a stained-glass swan, a sunset, a dragon. She cuts, jigsaws, and solders the windows together on her dining room table. A few of them hang for sale in the little sandwich shop she owns down by the boardwalk. She borrowed the money, five thousand dollars, from her ex to buy the hole-in-the-wall deli because her father refused to help. Poppop does not believe in unearned money.

To pay her ex back, and then just because she enjoys it, Gail also runs a route for Wise potato chips. She's the only woman with a delivery truck, the only woman with a route. She jogs in 5K road races against men. She dates a hairy cyclist, Ernie, who shaves his legs to reduce the pain from his road rash every time he crashes. Gail's the coolest person we know, and she's talked Mom into going out again after Mom's attack, at night.

The Red Bank Rockers are playing at Wonder Bar in Asbury Park. Between sets, Gail introduces Mom to the band's towering front man, Clarence Clemons, and after his show he promises to join them for a drink.

By most accounts, Clarence is a gentle, generous giant, not harmless by any means but inordinately open, and the man gets around. Most Jerseyans at this time along this stretch of the shore, from Sea Bright to Sea Girt, have a Clarence story. Whether or not it's true matters little. Clarence revels in legend.

Open a page, any page, of his memoir, *Big Man: Real Life & Tall Tales*, written with Don Reo, and you can see how Clarence nudges fact toward make-believe, and, too, how he put to good use his fair share of women, among them his five wives. Clarence can't seem to help it. He has an easy, winning way, with women and men. You get a sense of that from the iconic *Born to Run* cover, where Bruce will forever be leaning up against the Big Man's backside, pushing Clarence out of the frame.

As the Boss writes in the foreword for *Big Man*, where Clarence walks, *the world conforms to his presence.* That's not entirely true, not for a Black man in white America. Not then, not now. As Clarence himself notes, *The horn helped. I was softer when I played the horn, and that made them feel safe. Otherwise I felt I was just big and black and scary.*

At Wonder Bar, Clarence draws Mom out, after dark, Clarence along with her insistent sister.

Near the sandy edge of the Eastern Seaboard, in a bar by the dirty beach in winter, Clarence is all those things he says—soft, safe, big, Black, and scary—and then some. On every stage they graced together, Clarence and Bruce played up these very qualities, because they were trying to create, on command and for a paying audience, a real American moment. You can't tell a true American story without confronting race face-fucking-first.

And Clarence is no fool. He knows he's being used, if gently, by these two sisters, in the same way Bruce uses him, as a symbol, as a foil. Clarence just can't know the specifics, that this is some kind of half-assed, race-based, poor-white-woman's version of do-it-yourself cognitive behavioral therapy.

Even if Clarence did know and didn't approve, he'd get over it. There are reasons to believe Clarence Clemons is a man who doesn't care to hold a grudge. America won't allow it—not unless it's shtick and you're Laurence Tureaud, aka Mr. T—and so Mom, Gail, and Clarence enjoy that drink.

The sisters sip their vodka gimlets, and Clarence asks if they're twins. They shrug and smile. Lie and say yes. A little later, Mom asks Clarence to dance.

At six feet five inches, Clarence is no tiny dancer. He's a snapper foot shuffler. A horn player, he's smooth with his fingers and hands, his lips and tongue. From the hips down, he's clownish. You can see him ham it up for the music video he shot with Jackson Browne for their hit single, "You're a Friend of Mine." In it, Daryl Hannah, an audience of one, lies on a living room couch, weirdly water-coloring the intimate concert scene.

But at Wonder Bar, the scene's raucous. This is Jersey, after all. Yet Clarence is calming. He's a charmer, and he could clobber everyone in the place. Just like that, on comes some slow song. I imagine it's Springsteen's "My Hometown." Why not. Clarence and Mom sway together in time, and Mom shivers at first. When Clarence asks if she's cold, Mom doesn't answer, or answers by burrowing into him, 'cause she's right back in that night, ground wet, dark. She's falling into big Clarence, feels safe for the first time in what feels like forever. This, while my brothers and I are at Gail's house with our stand-in babysitter, Richie Serafino, because the teenage girl who usually watches us has a date of her own.

• • •

Whatever the color of their skin, many poor Americans— which is to say, the poor citizens of the richest nation in the history of civilization—but especially poor young Americans, feel owed. That's how I felt as a teenager. I felt fully justified lying, cheating, and stealing, because when I looked around, I saw what most other Americans were in possession of, and I felt not entitled but cheated. Robbed. I imagine the young man who assaulted Mom felt something similar. And fifteen-year-old Richie, our substitute babysitter, lives this owed attitude—long before I would grow to unknowingly copy it—and it makes him cool, and it makes him cruel.

Richie's a shore rat. A survivor. Like us, he's a poor Jersey boy, half Italian, whose dad doesn't live with him. But Richie's dad's around. Everyone calls him Jetty. We don't know why. We've met him, and Jetty's cooler than cool. He founded The Surfrider, second ever surf shop in Jersey, and he's been bad-mouthing Ron Jon down in Ship Bottom ever since. A bunch of sellouts, he says. Says they've commodified surf.

Richie's got an older girlfriend. She's sixteen, and she lets him drive her T-top Pontiac Firebird Trans Am, brand new and white as a bedsheet. She's brown-skinned and brown-haired. Italian and Catholic and gorgeous.

Richie likes cars. He quizzes us on makes and models, and I've gotten okay at identifying them. When I get one wrong, he punches me in my arm so hard that a hard knot rises instantly under my skin. Dead arm, he calls it, and my arm does die for a minute. Goes numb clear down to my fingertips. Says it's good for me. Makes me tough. More like a man. Not so gay. Or I'm forced to eat Earthstar's dry cat food, which tastes like bonemeal cardboard. Richie's big on education. He's teaching us how to curse properly, though we can't tell Mom or Gail, unless we want to get locked in the basement. We say dick, pussy, shit. We say fuck, ass, cunt.

My brothers and I are back on the rust-colored sectional couch, at Gail's, not on the other one at our house.

We've been told to sit fucking still, not to fucking move, or fucking else. There's no documentation of this—it's all hearsay—no report of investigation, and there never will be, not unless you consider this account as the next best thing.

At our house we have a couch just like Gail's. Six rearrangeable squares, plushly cushioned, very 1970s. Mom's is maroon, she might even call it merlot, and my education will continue there. But right now, we're on Gail's burnt-orange version, and Maria has burrowed a tunnel system into a few of the sections, a system she uses as a ferret latrine, and where she'll birth her babies in a few months.

Some portion of me—and sometimes I think it's most of me—will forever be on one or the other of those two sectional couches. It's as if I myself am sectional.

There are a few different mes scattered around this time and this place—circa 1984 Jersey Shore. I have a hard time piecing them together, making them fit. That's what this, all this, is, I suppose.

• • •

We're watching MTV. Gail was an early adopter of cable, and MTV's always on. Let's pretend it's Clarence and Jackson Browne in "You're a Friend of Mine," the one I've already mentioned, where Daryl Hannah water-colors the scene as it plays out. What she renders looks little like what we see, and a few years later, in 1992, at the end of their relationship, Browne and Hannah have a domestic dispute—she's leaving him for JFK Jr.—and Hannah ends up in the hospital.

Or maybe it's Michael Jackson's "Wanna Be Startin' Somethin'"—though I have no memory of a video for that song—or could be Suzanne Vega singing "Luka." Whatever it is, it's cut off—power goes out. Everything's dark all at once.

Shawn starts simpering. Dane's angry. And Richie, who is nowhere to be seen, has a friend over, some other young guy. He has no features, this friend, not that I recall, and it's possible I've imagined him. He's just a vague presence—all but absolutely absent—and a voice. For all I know, the friend could be God.

Richie bursts into the darkened living room. He moans. He works summers at the Haunted Mansion on the boardwalk—that is, before it burns down—where my brothers and I have been horrified. Staged there is a Lizzie Borden scene, Lizzie holding a bloody ax all set to chop her parents to bits. Teenagers who work there, boardwalk rats all, dress in costume and climb the walls, but they're not allowed to touch you. Richie's a werewolf, the most coveted job a kid can have at the boardwalk. This is like that. Except Richie has bare thighs. There's a black woolly wedge at his crotch, wolf-like, and I don't understand that it's hair not fur.

My brothers and I have few men in our lives, and certainly

not half-naked men. Richie's penis dangles down. I don't know if it's huge or if it's that, at seven years old, I'm small.

Richie jumps about the living room, monkey-like, moaning and shouting, I'm the devil! He bounds on the couch next to us in the dark. I'm the devil! His penis bounces all over, getting bigger. I'm the devil! I'm the devil! That dangle between his legs, I feel perversely compelled to call it his penus.

After a time—a time that maybe amounts to ten seconds but that has felt to me, my entire life, like a lifetime—the voice of the disembodied friend says, Richie, you are a crazy son-of-a-bitch. Come on, leave the kids alone. You're scaring them. Can't you see they're crying? Put your damn pants back on. Jesus.

And this is how my molestation—ongoing for months or years, I can't know—gets its start.

• • •

My first orgasms, there with Richie, are dry. It's something of a circle jerk. Richie, my little brothers, and me. Dane and Shawn, given their ages, are less involved.

When I come, nothing comes out. My penus gasps like a goldfish out of water.

My body isn't mature enough yet to make semen. But at the time, Richie doesn't recognize this. He just says I'm doing it wrong, and he punches me.

• • •

Pop music means the world to us and MTV made it so. It's the year of Van Halen's 1984 and The Eurythmics' 1984 (For the Love of Big Brother). Of Prince's Purple Rain. Chaka Khan feels for us. Sting plays his last concert with The Police at the end of the Synchronicity tour. Some of us sing along with Madonna's "Like a Virgin" not knowing what a virgin is, or watch the music video for Pat Benatar's "We Belong" wondering how many teeth she has in her mouth. Other things, outside of pop music, happen. Mom and Gail and their friends talk about some movie. The movie stars Shirley MacLaine, Debra Winger, Jack Nicholson, Danny DeVito, Jeff Daniels, and John Lithgow. The movie's based on a book by Larry McMurtry. The father from *The Shining* plays a retired astronaut, and just saying the movie's title makes Mom weepy. I think it must be some kind of *Bambi* but for grown-ups, where the doe gets shot and dies, because what I hear everyone calling the movie is *Terms of End Deer Mint*.

• • •

My informal education—as I've said—starts with language. Swear words. This is how we're groomed. We're talked into it. Taken into confidence. Tested. We're told things, things most adults don't want us to know. After the telling comes the showing. The more taboos in a household, the greater the points of entry for someone like Richie. Hard to know how long the initial phase lasts. Some night after the "I'm the devil" episode, the lessons progress to pictures.

My brothers and I passed some sort of test. Richie jumped around Gail's living room half-naked, swinging his penus in our faces—I'm just gonna keep spelling it that way, so get used to it, get over it, or give up on me and go do something else—and a month or more later, Gail walks over to Richie's, knocks on his door. When he answers—is there fear in his eyes?—she asks if he can babysit. This Saturday.

You want me to babysit again?

If you can.

Yeah, sure. I did okay the last time?

None of the boys choked to death or got kidnapped, right? But there's one thing.

Ah, I—

Maria just had her babies, so you got to be careful with them. They're each worth a couple hundred dollars. So please make sure the boys don't handle them too much.

Got it. Not a fucking problem, I mean—shit, sorry.

And you need to do better watching your mouth around the boys. If you can't clean up your language, we'll have to find some other substitute sitter.

• • •

We're on the couch at Gail's. MTV's on. There's no friend over this time. It's just Richie, my brothers, and me, plus the ferrets, with their sweet ferret funk—musky and cunty. That's what Richie says anyway. We tell him we get to take one of the six ferret babies home in a couple days. We're going to name her Bandit.

Richie calls my brothers and me into Gail's bedroom. He wants us to see something he found. Know what this is?

I've already seen the thing he's holding. Like Richie, I found it once upon a time in Gail's bedside drawer, and she told me what it was called. She got it from a cop, a leather-wrapped leaded ball at one end. She keeps it in her nightstand, just to be safe, along with a four-inch jackknife, the red handle imbedded with a prowling black panther.

I say, A slapjack.

Very good, he says, and he goes to punch me but stops short.

I flinch anyway.

That's two, he says. And he hits me twice, first hard, then harder.

Ow.

You know, your Aunt Gail, she's some kinky-ass bitch. Why don't you gohead take a look under the bed.

I shake my head no.

It's not only the bed, the undersides of which have been horrifying since we saw *Poltergeist* (the way Tobe Hooper, again, taps directly into a kid's worst fears) on video the year before. There's something about Richie's affect. It's not menacing. It's fake. Manipulative—that's what I'd call it all these years later—he's leading me toward some end he has in mind.

Adults always keep them under the bed, he says. Get down, take a look.

Keep what?

Go on. You'll see.

• • •

Curse words were first. Fuck cunt shit. Next came nudity. Richie's full-frontal penus in our faces. What follows is porn. Pictures of men and women, women and women, of all different colors and combinations, coupling, and tripling, and quadrupling, in ways I never could've imagined. Here were adult bodies like our kid bodies—only bigger, hairier—opening and extending and inserting one into another. Fitting together like slippery Tinkertoys. It was strange and exciting. Come to find, women had an opening under them, a kind of wet pocket. And men could grow and extend themselves to tuck into that pocket. And adults—I don't know if you know this but adults in the 1980s at least—have hair absolutely everywhere.

• • •

I do as told, diving halfway under the bed. There is a neat stack of magazines.

Richie tells me to pull them on out. Go on, they won't bite.

When I hesitate—there's something off about all this, something wrong—I'm punched, hard, in the hamstring. I yelp but I don't cry. Instead, I put an arm around the stack and heave the magazines fanning out from under the bed.

There's one I recognize, *Playboy*, which Gail gets in the mail and is kept in a basket in her bathroom with *Rolling Stone*.

Some others that splay out from under the bed: *Color Climax*, *Juggs*, *Oui*.

Gail's got good taste. This one here, at shit's French. Oo-we. Means yes. No girl knows more about sex than a French girl. And, wow, look at this. September issue of *Penthouse*. Lemme show you Miss America. Lookit here. At's Vanessa Williams. She's part Black, but you ask me, she looks Sicilian. This magazine's owned by a paisan. Bob Guccione. Richest Italian in the U.S. Also makes movies. Some Roman thing called *Caligula*. Emperor of Rome butters up his prick and fucks everyone up the ass. I haven't seen it yet, just heard about it. In Rome, adults had sex with kids. Boy, girl, didn't matter. The Romans were some horny motherfuckers, man. Speaking of kids. Look at this girl right here. No fucking way at bitch's eighteen. Traci Lords. Good lord. Girl right there's as old as my girl. If that. Here. This here's the centerfold. And here's what you do with a centerfold. You lay it out, get a good look, and then you take your pecker out. Gohead. All three a you boys. Just like you would take a pee. But don't you dare fucking pee! Here, I'll get mine out to show you. You take out your peepee and you stroke it. No peeing now. You boys know the Billy Squier song. It's on the radio every ten minutes. Stroke me, stroke me, stroke, stroke. You kinda make a loose fist. At's it. And you pump up and down. At's it. Stroke. Stroke.

• • •

At first I'm sent to St. James Catholic elementary in Red Bank, but when Mom finds a job as a clerk at Cohen's Deli in Highlands, I begin third grade at a school closer to her work.

So she can collect welfare and afford our tuition at the Catholic school on the hill, Our Lady of Perpetual Help, she's paid under the table by the owner, Al.

Mom and Gail know better, but Al's shady dealings, helping them at first, will end up costing them.

Al lives over the deli with his wife and two boys. They don't celebrate Christmas. Al has a reputation as a loan shark, one who demands a reasonable weekly vigorish on his advances, and I'm not sure what any of this means but I like the sound of it. Vigorish, vig for short. Al wears brown suits and lets us play all day, every day, in his office.

While I'm in school, Dane and Shawn spend their days at the deli. Sometimes they're tended to by our regular babysitter, Rachel, a mouthy teenage Highlands townie, who in winter likes to deposit us in the empty lot beside the laundromat, so we can stand under the vents and be showered with warm steam. It's beautiful. She calls it Cloud 9.

Walking home one day from OLPH, I have a few heavy dollars in quarters weighing down my pocket, stolen from Mom's jewelry box.

I stop at the drugstore and spend a while spinning the display rack of earrings. I've been planning this for weeks. I settle on a pair, two wire-wreathed whorls painted gray. They're stud versions of the hoop earrings Tina Turner will wear to the apocalypse in *Mad Max Beyond Thunderdome*. I can see them so vividly, over thirty years later, and so ugly—they looked more like car parts than jewelry—that it's hard to believe they still don't exist somewhere. But then, and there, I thought they were beautiful, the wiry way they threaded in on each other, and that Mom would love them.

Late now, and inspiring worry, I hustle in the direction of the deli. I pass the dark house where Mom bought a hot VCR, among the first of its kind, for next to nothing.

I reach the small crushed-shell lot beside the deli and my mom's rusted-out Plymouth Valiant. I hate the car that puts our poverty on display for the whole school each morning I'm dropped off, but I love its chrome bumper. I pop a rust bubble with my fingertip, and look up.

Coming at me, coming for me, from the far side of the deli, is old Bill Kolakowski, a massive man, maybe in his fifties, his brushy gray beard smoke-yellowed, his long gray hair greased back. Same as always, he wears oil-stained overalls over big bulb-toed boots, the steel reinforcement flashing through the torn leather. His most frightening feature is his face, bumped and mottled, an ugly topography of angry acne scars.

My brothers and I love his son, Billy, a gentle beast of a young man as vast as his dad, but always clean-shaven, hair cut high and tight, always happy to see us and toss us around like loaves of warm bread. But Billy's gone, shipped off with the U.S. Marines, and here is his frightening father.

I am sure—in a prescient way I'd never been before and maybe never have been since—that the father is determined to abduct me. My fear is so palpable, so sudden and so certain, that I almost wet myself. I dash behind the long chassis of my mom's Valiant, climb under the car, and, cowering—smelling the damp of the basement where I'm bound to be locked away, tasting the dust of the closet where I'm destined to be tied—I pinch my penus and try not to pee.

Those broken boots, huge, scuff eternally by, in the narrow length of daylight between the rear tires, slow, then stop. I hold my breath and cover my eyes, whimpering, Mommy mommy mommy, as quietly as I can. Voluntarily, I let go my bladder. The warmth. The wet. The release. A relief supreme. Maybe the nearest that most seven-year-old boys—though not me—get to the sensation of orgasm.

After a forever moment, the boots scuff once, twice, and, then, those boots shamble on. When gone, when I can no longer hear the scratch-crunch of them, I think of lies I might tell my mom about my wet pants, hoping the earrings in my pocket will save me from a spanking. Dane's the bedwetter, not me, and Shawn's a night screamer, dreaming always of the same rabid black dog. Me, I wake every morning sick to my stomach, dry heaving into the toilet, begging to be kept home from OLPH. Mom's sympathy is short on these mornings, as she, far outnumbered and on her own, dresses, feeds, and harangues the three of us.

If your stomach hurts, she tells me, take a poop. You're not missing any school.

• • •

Easter weekend 1985. Mom and Gail, my brothers and me, we fly to Florida to spend the holiday with Nana and Poppop.

This is no vacation, not really. We can't afford vacations. This is recon bought on credit. Mom and Gail have been talking about moving us down here. Cost of living's far cheaper than Jersey, where, in order to qualify for food stamps, Mom works under-the-table.

An honest person warped by the welfare system, Mom rarely lies and yet she feels compelled to cheat. As an American woman, she has less earning power to begin with. Divorce is designed to make financial matters worse. Mom blames our father for his felonies. Yet she's forced, by the fallout from his tax fraud, to commit tax fraud. These are the sorts of moral contortions poverty imposes on Americans, poor parents especially, and none more so than single mothers.

Mom solo. Raising three young boys, she can't work full-time to feed, clothe, and house said boys, all while affording the childcare full-time work demands. Not in this man's America, no, sir, not unless the full-time work is compensated off the books.

Compromises like these set up such folks, already compromised, to fall further prey—as Gail will find out soon enough—prey to the lawless, prey to the law. This is often represented as the poor decision-making of the poor. But when choosing between least worst outcomes, the only choice is a bad choice. It's either that or the decision that'll prove far worse.

The shit choice my father makes, to cheat taxes, results in a bad plot that ruins his marriage to my mother. Divorce requires she work nights delivering pizzas. Puts her in harm's way. There, she's more likely to get attacked. Meanwhile, my brothers and I, reared in a fatherless home, become—after adjusting for ethnicity, education, and household income— twice as likely, at least, to be sexually abused.

Pederasts are especially put off by dads. It's not hard to imagine why. There is a couple hundred thousand years of aggressive, and possessive, human evolution standing resolutely behind a father. Fatherless sons are easier pickings. In a patriarchy, mothers are simply not as intimidating.

Our father fucks up, and Mom herds us out the front door for the final time. The instant the door latches behind us, we're poorer. Mom and I, along with my two brothers forever scraping by, have been paying the price ever since. And we're not alone. Quite the opposite. We've got too much miserable company.

One in four American kids lives in a fatherless home. The detriments to the development of these children are devastating. This is how bad fortune is manufactured and distributed in America. This is how the American Dream dies along the roadside.

Divorce doesn't necessarily cause Mom to be prone to assault—though there's some evidence to suggest that it does—but divorce, with zero doubt, directly affects her financial security. Less money does make her more of a target. It's that easy. The cause, poverty, and the effect, abuse, are so intimately united in this country that they're nearly the same damn thing. Poverty is abuse.

• • •

Put my brothers and me beside three boys raised in a home with both biological parents—the biological part is, sad to say, statistically significant—and the odds are better that my brothers and I are shorter. We're the ones who're beaten. We're the fat ones. We get molested. We quit school. We run away. We do drugs. Commit crimes. Do hard time. End up homeless. We go crazy. We get sick. We kill ourselves. We die young, just like the real cool pool players hanging out at the Golden Shovel in the Gwendolyn Brooks poem. Never mind that we're whiteboys.

We are, on the whole, bound to fuck shit up and bad, for ourselves and those around us. All this puts a terrible strain on Mom, and on the nation. There is a line, albeit winding, from fatherlessness to our failing infrastructure.

Do I blame my unavailable father for our nation's failings? When my vigilance falters on the back roads of rural Michigan, and I slam blindly through a gaping rut in asphalt older than I am, do I scream, Fuck you, Dad! No. No, I do not. I see him as no all-consuming villain. More often than not, I imagine him as a troubled teen running the tables with Danny DeVito in the billiard halls of Asbury Park. But that's another story altogether. Do I blame our father for all our family fallout? I didn't. I didn't care, really. He quit on us early enough that he never achieved the status of a presence to be remembered, never mind forgotten. He was absence. Emptiness. A hollow, one not even waiting to be filled, not knowingly anyway.

But the more time I spend investigating the issue, the more I realize how much blame is assignable. How determining a hole can be. Our father's departure is an early grave he dug for my brothers and me, and it's up to us—not entirely but mostly—to keep from falling in. That, or diving in face-fucking-first.

• • •

Even in our increasingly secular world, the sins of the father are still visited upon the sons and daughters both, though study after study shows that sons feel the loss of a father far more acutely. Daughters raised by single mothers are more resilient, for the durations of their lives, than are their brothers—and I'm speaking here not for the confounding predeterminations of chromosomal sex but for the alignments of our identified gender—partly because a presence, rather than an absence, offers an available model to emulate.

I'm coming to learn that no single sin is greater, more fu-

rious, than the simple, unforgiving—if not unforgivable—sin
of leaving.

• • •

You could argue, a bit lazily, that the desertion of one's children fits under sloth—translated from the Latin word *acedia*,
literally "without care."

I say desertion—an omitted sin, also a sin of omission—
deserves to stand on its own. There should be eight deadly
sins, and desertion can be considered the deadliest sin of all.

I could even go as far as to say that desertion, not disobedi-
ence, is the original sin—what some theologians call ancestral
sin, a doctrine that predates Christ—but I won't because I'm a
heretic Catholic now devoutly agnostic.

Celsus, the ancient Greek philosopher reasoning against
Christianity in his polemic *True Doctrine*, written circa 175 AD,
attributes the idea of ancestral sin, the bequest of faults, to a
priest of Apollo or of Zeus, that the *mills of the gods grind slowly,
even to children's children, and to those who are born after them.*

We are the inheritors of our God, or gods, and desertion is
the first sin committed against us by God.

The Old Testament—that wholesale copying of the Hebrew Tanakh—is a morality play starring a thoroughly sinful
God. And God's first sin?

Leaving Adam alone in Eden.

Out of His guilt for this sin, God creates Eve, so that Eve
and Adam may be together in desertion.

Desertion will also be the final sin committed by God,
when He disappears from our lives for good, if He hasn't already. This makes desertion the ultimate sin. Like God in the
apocalyptic book of Revelation, desertion is the alpha and the
omega, first and last. And we are all, after all, made in God's
image. The best available copy. Or is God made in our image?
I can never keep those two straight in my head.

• • •

As with God, so too will desertion be our final act.

Desertion is the last thing every last one of us will do. And we will all do it on our own.

How sad a thought, that. Strange, too.

There's some small creature comfort in this. A kinship.

For all of us, our final experience, our last letting go, is one thing we will all be certain to share. Alone together. Desertion is a true universal.

And—if you humor me one more moment, before I return us to the personal story, because what's of most interest to you is the hardest on me, and these bits here are meditative, transcendental almost, moments of highfalutin uplift before we redescend to the harsh reality on the ground—the doctrine of ancestral sin may be seen as the prototype for the theory of evolution.

The faults of Celsus become Charles Darwin's mutations. Our faults and our mutations both threaten to do us in, to kill us, to damn us to extinction, until they don't. In that case, they may make us stronger. For the mills of the genes grind slowly, even to our children's children, and to those who are born after them.

What matters most is not the fault or the mutation handed down. What matters most is whether or not the receiving generation has the wherewithal to turn a troublesome inheritance into some small advantage.

• • •

Three weeks before we visit our grandparents for Easter 1985, a funnel cloud tears ass through South Venice, Florida. Sucks up whole homes and businesses. Spits them out as splinters a mile or more away. Does more damage, in financial costs at that time, than any other Sunshine State twister. Two people die. The tornado clears a wide swath not far from Poppop and Nana's low-slung, one-story ranch house built of brick. Wolf huffed and puffed, Poppop says, but didn't blow our house in. No, sir.

In his old, gray Buick the color of a battleship, Poppop tours us proudly around the devastation. This is what we do instead of going to Disney. Mom rides shotgun. Gail's in back beside me, Dane, and Shawn. My little brothers are asleep in minutes. Their heads loll. Nearly tumble off their necks into their laps with every turn of the car.

He's a fighter, Poppop is, a survivor, and he wants people to know it. Trailer parks didn't stand a chance, he's saying through cigarette smoke he blows out the driver-side window. Where we shop, right there. Or did.

A once-sprawling Publix market is a muddled mountain range of building material piled high with old, sodden groceries getting sunbaked. I can practically see how it happened, and from above, how the tornado gouged its cloudy God thumb—turned disapprovingly down—into the blue eye of an unsuspecting planet Earth.

We turn north, up Tamiami Trail. Mom and Gail like Sarasota better than Venice. Would put some distance—half an hour—between father and daughters.

Healthy for you and me both, Poppop says, his wet guffaws unsettling his dentures.

Dane blinks awake, yawns, falls back asleep against sleeping Shawn.

Gail says she could open up a sandwich shop in any one a these here strip malls.

We visit a few neighborhoods. Palmy and narrow, they're disturbing. Houses like cigarette cartons. Practically campers on cinder blocks.

Lot of these places don't let kids in, Poppop says. Royal Palms and Venetian Lakes're both fifty-five and older.

Mom and Gail are even too young, I say from the back seat. They're thirty-five. Poppop thinks this amusing.

What? I ask.

Dad, Mom says, Gail and me've been thirty-five for some time now.

Yeah, Gail says. Years. Though Shest's a more mature thirty-five.

What's that aspose to mean? I ask.

We drive through Sarasota Bay Mobile Home Park, which does take kids.

Kids' toys—once-bright plastics, solid, turned drab and translucent by the sun—are scattered everywhere.

Was the tornado here?

When I'm told no, I still don't like the look of the place. When I ask why the houses are so long and skinny, Mom says they're called mobile homes.

Mobile's right, Poppop says. Specially in a twister.

Dad!

What. Be fun for the boys. Just like Dorothy in *Wizard of Oz*.

Jay, Mom says, how'd you like to live in one a those?

I don't know, I say.

$$\bullet \ \bullet \ \bullet$$

Back at Poppop's, we meet a man Nana tells us to call Uncle Don. He's not to be confused with our Uncle Donald, whom we know and love. Like us, Don's visiting from Jersey. Uncle Don is Mom and Gail's stepbrother. Kind of. They, too, are meeting this new Don for the first time.

Why haven't we never met him before? I ask Mom. Why haven't you?

He's got a hungry look, this Uncle Don does, and he's looking it hard at Mom. He cocks his head. Something in his red squint makes me reach out a hand to Mom.

Well, she says, careful, not looking in the direction of our new uncle, a brother by marriage. He's been—away.

Yeah, Uncle Don says. Away in Rahway. He winks a blood-shot eye. Big sis.

He's thirty-four years old, Uncle Don is. His eyebrows arch sharply. He's surprised, constantly. Reminds me of someone. Floppy hair. Wears cutoff shorts, button-down shirt unbuttoned all the way down. He has muscles, Uncle Don does, a hairy chest. His feet are bare. He's very pale. Ain't allowed to drink no booze whatsoever, he says, so he sips one of Nana's off-brand diet colas from a highball glass in a way that arouses suspicion.

We're told to stay clear of him.

We want to watch TV. But Uncle Don claims the living room, ignoring the muted screen, downing sodas, staring at the wall over the kitchen counter. There, two deer hooves, mounted on ovals of oak, present arms. Poppop's bolt-action rifle. Supported by what's left of the buck Poppop shot with the firearm.

Seeing Uncle Don stare at this display, I'm confused. I ask where the horns are. I'm told they're called antlers. I ask, Why's there only two feet? Where's the other two?

Everybody thinks this question's funny, everyone but Uncle Don and me.

They're poking out the other side of the wall, Poppop says, 'long with the tail.

When I look, there's nothing on the other side but wall.

Back in the living room, staring at Uncle Don, I say, Got it!

What, Mom says.

He looks like the oldest boy in The Partridge Family, I say. Only older.

Uncle Don says, Hell's The Partridge Family?

• • •

Easter morning, we don't bother with church. We have an egg hunt on the lanai. I win. Shoving my brothers out the way. The eggs are plastic. I pop them open. Some have money inside. A quarter. A nickel. A penny. I'm told to share and I do as told, grumbling. Always being told to share, I can't ever get good at it, sharing. I hate it. Don't know why. I just do. I want to keep everything I have all for myself, always.

Our plastic baskets are filled with plastic grass.

Poppop and Nana smoke for breakfast. Poppop's packs are discount Basic, bought by the carton. Nana smokes twiggy Virginia Slims. They look too thin to be believable. Like she's pretending to smoke, sucking on a straight white wire.

We eat chocolate bunnies big as our arms but hollow. I find the hollowness devastating. Strikes me as a scam all adults pull on all kids everywhere. Year after year. Happy fucking Easter. Here's an empty bunny. It's mostly air. Enjoy.

I break mine into milk-chocolate smithereens. I eat the candy eyes, the ears, the cotton-ass tail.

We down jellybeans by the fistful, but our fists are small. As a way to get even with the adults, I pull a fast one on Dane, trade my row of impossibly yellow marshmallow Peeps for his Cadbury Creme Egg, wonderfully disgusting, so sweet it makes me gag between bites. Even I—a fat nine-year-old getting fatter—can stomach just one or two a year. But two's better than one, and Dane's a sucker for Peeps, which have always seemed to me to be coated in sand.

● ● ●

The morning's going from warm to hot. Already eighty degrees. Some blue sky between towers of cotton-swab cloud. After a brunch, following our candy breakfast, of scrambled eggs and bacon, English muffins, their crannies spackled with margarine nearly as yellow as the Peeps, we spend hours cannonballing into the pool, a miraculous in-ground rectangle of blue marcite with tile trim.

Poppop asks if I like the pool.

No, I tell him, I *love* it.

Pool like this, Poppop says, is just like the ones Tony was putting in. Before things turned south.

I ask, Who's Tony again?

We're told we're going to get cramps but we never do get cramps. I let Mom and Gail know I'm not returning home. I hate Jersey. I hate Catholic school. I hate the Franciscan sisters in brown and Father Dave and his jug ears. I hate my one green tie and one pair of too-tight slacks, always stained. I hate it all to hell. My mouth underwater, I add, It's shitty. My inaudible words bubble. Shitty, I bubble. I bubble, Tony.

• • •

Poppop's telling me he invented the molly bolt but someone beat him to the patent.

Was gonna name it the Dolly bolt, after your mother's mother. Lemme show you something else I thought up. He points. See how those pine needles fall down, from that pine tree up there? See how those stabbing bastards poke right through the screen?

Where, I don't see.

Open your eyes. Right there. Screen that's the top of the lanai. See how those needles poke right through to get stuck?

Yeah, I see now.

Well it's hell to get them out, without me falling off my ladder, straight through the screen and, splash, into the pool.

I laugh. That'd be funny.

Maybe to you. He regards me. Can I trust you?

I shrug.

'Cause if I tell you, and you go blabbedy-blabbing about it, someone might steal my idea, make my million bucks. Know what they say about loose lips?

I shake my head.

No, don't suppose you do.

When he goes quiet, I say, Tell me, Poppop. Tell me, tell me. I zip my lips.

Swear on your mother you'll not tell a living soul.

Without parting my lips, I mumble, Hm hmar.

What? Swear on your mother.

Hom hm mh-hm.

Okay, he says. You can unzip. He points to a pole—metal rectangle attached to one end—leaning against the exterior wall of the house. He says, I made it.

A pole?

Not just a pole. Here. Show you.

We visit the pole. He hands it to me, proudly. What do you think?

Why's it got a driver license screwed on it?

That's a license plate. Careful. I ground down the top edge so it's razor-sharp. He runs a finger over it. Ouch! He winks. Just kidding. But it will cut you. Lemme show you how it works. You take it like this. Press the sharp edge up to the screen there. Gentle, so's not to slice through. Otherwise I got to get up there, on my ladder, to replace it, and I fall into the pool.

I laugh.

You think that's funny, idea of your old poppop falling in the pool.

I nod, laughing.

Well not today. He returns to his demonstration. See, you swipe along. Easy. See. Needles get shaved right off. Just like whiskers at the barber. *Shave and a haircut,* he croons, *sham-poo.* Know that song?

I shake my head and have a dizzy moment. The screened-in top of the lanai is the cheek of the sky's face, and all the poking-down pine needles are whiskers on that face. It's monstrous. Could be all the sugar. I shake it off and manage to say, Neat.

Neat? Hell of a lot better than neat. It's practical genius. Best kind. Need to get me a patent for it. Your other grandfather, Ed, Tony's father, he's got a few patents to his name, you know. One for some dingle bells. Bells of St. Nicholas. Made his fortune. Before he lost it. I get mine approved, they can start selling it on Marge's home shopper program. Make my million. When I die, leave what's left to you and your mom. How'd that be?

Okay.

What should we call it? He shakes his pole. My invention here. Mind you, this just a mockup.

I shrug. Sky Razor?

Sky Razor. Hmh. Sky Razor. Maybe. I been calling it the Screen Shaver. What do you think a that? Screen Shaver. Would you wanna buy one? Might cut you a deal.

• • •

By afternoon, Uncle Don and Poppop start sniping at each other through the wide sliding glass door, that or the kitchen window opening onto the lanai.

I feel the meanness strung up like a low clothesline between them. I feel it under my stomach. A need to pee that never goes away. I don't want to use the bathroom, walk past Uncle Don, so I piss in the pool. The warmth that fills my shorts is bliss. Then it's gone. Everything's colder after.

• • •

Why don't you, Don, Poppop's saying from the lanai, just go on ahead. Help yourself to another a your mother's Cokes.

They're not really Cokes, I say to no one, and no one cares. They're colas.

Won't mind if I do, Gussy. Don stumbles around the kitchen. Slamming cabinets, yanking drawers. Gussy won't mind if I do. Don's voice has changed. His words slur. He sounds funny. "Gussy" sounds like "Gushy."

Don isn't really Nana's son. And Nana's not really Mom's mom. Mom's mom died at age forty-four, on 24 May 1970, when Mom was twenty-four, and Poppop remarried within minutes. It was something of an outrage—the assumption that Poppop and Marge were having an affair—but mom's mom had been sick for a couple of years. Pancreatic cancer. When Marge's sister died young, before she met Poppop,

Marge took custody of Don. And Don, we're told, has been bad since the day his mother died. A criminal. A thief. A jailbird. A murderer.

Gail says he stabbed a baker in Phoenix, a jeweler in Jersey.

Shut up, Gail, Mom says. He did not kill no baker.

Okay, just a jeweler then. Far as we know.

A cripple, Poppop says. Poor fella, guy name a Gregov. Wife called his jewelry shop, in Cliffside Park think it was, every fifteen damn minutes. What the papers said. Worried he'd get robbed, have a stroke. Poor sonavabitch never missed not a one of her calls. You 'magine? Every fifteen minutes? For six years? Always answered. That is, till Marge's sweet son, Don, in there, paid him a call.

Oh, Gussy, that was ages in the past.

Yeah, says Poppop. In the past, with an ice pick. Poppop punches a fist against his chest, over his heart.

Nana says, Don paid his debt, Gus.

Not to us he didn't. Not yet. To Mom and Gail, Poppop says, Owes us for his bail bond.

Not his fault my sister, God rest her, died on him like she done. Only thing worse an a boy without a father's one with no mother.

I watch to see if Nana looks at me. She doesn't; Mom does.

So I do what I can, Nana says. When I can. Why he's here with us now.

Poppop tells Mom and Gail that Don was released on parole for the Gregov murder back in June. In that time he's racked up three new arrests. Last one, month ago in Jersey, was for armed robbery and assault. With a firearm. On a cop. Got no idea how or why they let him out again, but they did, on April Fools' Day. Joke's on us, I think. After we posted his bail. And here he is. Drinking all Marge's Cokes. All so she and him can share an Easter.

First one together in forever. Since he was just a boy, I think it was. It's the Christian thing to do, Gus.

Christian thing would be nail his crooked ass to the cross. One beside Jesus.

Oh, Gus. You're such a heathen.

I listen to all this from the pool, pretending I'm paying no attention. I don't know where Dane and Shawn are and I don't even want to know.

I'm told again—and with new emphasis—stay away from Don. Hear me?

Uncle Don, I correct, fascinated to have an honest-to-God killer, and presumably a jewel thief, for an uncle. Fucking rad, I bubble below the surface.

Mom asks, Where's your brothers?

I shrug and spit pool water.

Gail goes inside. A moment later, she yells, Shest!

We all run in to what's being called the Florida room.

• • •

I'm dripping. When I ask what's a Florida room, why's it called a Florida room, can you have a Florida room in New Jersey, I'm told that a Florida room's really just a second living room. In Jersey they call it a den.

Dane and Shawn have managed to make a mess of the strangest lamp—dangling in the Florida room—that any of us have ever seen. The lamp reminds me of the major award, a glowing fishnet leg, that the Old Man wins in *A Christmas Story*, only stranger. Greasier. R-rated. The warm lamp drips, like I do, onto the carpet.

At's a lamp? I say. At's not a lamp. Seems some sorta—I don't know what.

Oh, this messy thing, Marge says. It's only mineral oil. It'll wash. I hope.

The lamp's like a long birdcage, bronze, hanging low from the ceiling by a bronze chain. Instead of a bird it keeps a little bronze woman. Instead of bars there's monofilament line. The lamp's supposed to rain oil, oil that dribbles down the lines angling all around the lady. A red light shines hotly on her from above. As if she were a side order of fries. She stands nearly two feet tall in the slow rain. Knee-deep in plastic ferns. Her toga is off one shoulder. She's stuck flashing us her brass breast. Her tiny nipple twinkles.

Dane and Shawn are slick with oil. I'm sure they were reaching in, touching the woman, her ferns, her breast, a breast like we've seen in Gail's magazines, shown to us by Richie, a breast like we've seen on Mom, only bigger, less twinkly.

When I reach in my hand, I get whacked.

Ow.

Oh, Mom says. I'll give you ow.

When I go back to the lanai, Poppop waves me over. Hop up here, he says, patting his lap. Just like an Easter Bunny. He winks. A chubby Easter Bunny.

I climb onto his lap. I'm breathing Poppop's man atmosphere. Smells strange to me. Like a state I've never visited, somehow volcanic. Hawaii maybe. Smells of smoke, of Florida's sulfur water, eggy, and old armpit.

• • •

In Poppop's smoky lap on the lanai, I rub his scruffy chin, its satisfying grit. Like a bar of Lava soap.

What'd they do, he asks. They get into my Venus lamp?

I shrug.

In the dripping oil, I thought the woman was undressing to take a rain shower. But now I'm convinced the lamp woman is supposed to be from another planet. Venus. A brassy alien beamed down to Earth in that teleporter red light.

Or could be the plants around the woman's feet are Venus flytraps. Maybe she's about to be eaten by a hungry salad. All that oil, only thing missing is vinegar.

I don't say any of this—I don't think—I think I just think it.

Poppop reaches around me. Like he's going to hug me.

Poppop's not a hugger kind of a grampa though. He's more a kisser. Gives a troika of little pecks: smoky, spitty, scruffy. But he doesn't kiss me, not this time.

This time, he pinches one of the rolls of my stomach. There're four or five for him to choose from. He's grabbed the biggest roll. Not pinching gently but it doesn't hurt.

I say, Ow, anyway, and he lets go.

Getting fat there. Aren't you?

He wants an answer to this question.

I shrug.

Both you and your mother. Shouldn't be able to pinch more than an inch. You've about half a foot there. Belly like a pack a Hebrew National. What she feeding you?

I don't tell him that, at JCPenney, I've got to try on pants pulled from circle racks in the "husky" section. I fucking hate the "husky" section. Come time to pay, I stay far from the register. I hide in the center of a circle rack of fat pants for fat boys, fat. Mom's Penney's card never fucking works. She gets upset. First comes the yelling, then the crying. Everything I squeezed into—Suck in, she tells me in the changing room, suck in, as she wrestles my button, fights my fly; I am, Mom, I'm sucking far as I can—it all goes back on the fat racks. Why bother.

I don't say any of this either. All I do, sitting on Poppop's lap, is shrug again. I don't remember his question anyway.

Should start doing pushups, he says. Every day. Know how to do a pushup?

I shrug.

He hoists me onto my feet. Takes out his dentures, sets them beside the full ashtray.

On the pebbly patio floor of the lanai, Poppop does noisy pushups. He pushes up so hard and so fast, he's able to clap his hands together in the air beneath him before resetting them on the ground. He's an old man, his thin, gray hair falling forward, his thick but solid body straight and stiff. He's breathing hard. He counts after each clap.

I watch his dentures. Wait for the claps to somehow jump-start the teeth, set them chattering across the tabletop.

Poppop's up to twenty, twenty-one, he's going for forty, he says, when Don cracks open a new soda from the kitchen. We hear it fizz all over the fucking place.

Don's yelling, Ah fuck shit Christ bitch, where's the damn whatchacallit at? Gushy!

Poppop stops push-clapping.

I peek in. Tan cola foam falls all over Uncle Don's fingers. He pours what's left of the can into his glass. He sees me and raises a shushing finger to his lips. Then he says through the window, Grateful, Gushy, for all your generoshitty. Shit, I just say shitty? Mean generosity. Slip a the old fucking tongue. 'Scuse me, little man. Got a good gut on you, don'tcha. Here, want a ship?

I do want a ship. And a sip. And I want to hide. Bury my head in my bellybutton. It's wide and deep. I can sink in half a finger when I want to.

Back on the lanai, I ask Poppop if I can have a cola.

Poppop, catching his breath, wincing on his knees, says, First, drop on down here. Lemme see you gimme ten.

Ten?

Push, he says, breathing heavy. Don't have to clap.

Poppop climbs to his feet. He takes the long route up.

Standing, finally, he says, between huffs, into the kitchen window, Now, Don. Coke's on us. Long as you sure. Pay back your mother. Bail bond we posted—wadn't cheap. Seven hundred fifty dollars. Understand?

Uncle Don doesn't seem to understand. He sits back down on the couch, shaking off his wet hand. Wipes it on a cushion. Stares again into some middle distance, refocuses on the mounted rifle.

● ● ●

I don't imagine Uncle Don was thinking of Anton Pavlovich Chekhov just then, same way I sure as hell wasn't, but I can't help but think of Chekhov now, how he wrote, in a letter dated 1889 to Aleksandr Semenovich Lazarev, *One must never place a loaded rifle on the stage if it isn't going to go off. It's wrong to make promises you don't mean to keep.*

If not for the copies of old newspaper articles I have of the *Sarasota Herald-Tribune*, I'd think there was some chance I was making all of this up. 'Cause from a storyteller's perspective, it's almost too fucking good to be true. But from my vantage, in the ever-shifting present, it all feels too bad to be false. And unfortunately, the reports support my troubled memory.

But maybe I should let you know the rifle isn't loaded?

• • •

The TV, tuned to Home Shopping Club and its volume zeroed, shows a muted Bubblin' Bobbi, the host. She's peddling some sort of weird waffle iron thingamajig. You can put all kinds of different foods in. They all come out golden brown and delicious. I'm watching from behind the sliding glass door. I want one. I'm hungry. Poppop? I say. I get down and press my belly to the warm pebble flooring of the lanai. Like this?

And, Don, Poppop says. Breathing a little easier now, but not easy. Best start making plans to attend that hearing back in Jersey. Hear me? You don't, I'm out seventy-five hundred bucks. Can't afford to be losing that kinda income. Pension money worked hard my whole life for. Unlike some.

• • •

Nana's always nervous. Flighty, Mom says. A flibbertigibbet. Now, though, Nana's nearly effervescing. Her round, red-dye hairdo's like a fishbowl filled with Orange Crush sloshing all over the place. She's back on the lanai, having degreased Dane, Shawn, and the carpet. She's saying, Gus, what should I do with the—why you all sweaty? And breathing like that? You alright?

Poppop waves her off.

Nana fidgets in a new way, practically popping. You need your nitroglycerin?

No, Poppop says. Don't need no Goddamn nitroglycerin Goddamnit.

I abandon my pushup. Back in the pool, I pee. There isn't much pee left in me.

● ● ●

Our uncle Don may be an icepick killer out on parole but our poppop's an old soldier who helped save the world. A seaman who crewed aboard three—count them, three—different U.S. Navy ships downed in the Pacific during World War II. Poppop's fellow sailors tried calling him Unlucky Gussy. To this he gamely fired back, Lucky enough to've survive each sinking now wadn't I. We get hit, best do what I do. Otherwise, you might not be so lucky. And they did, they stuck close to Lucky Gussy.

In his Jersey civilian life after the war, Poppop's a proud trowel-carrying mason, an employee of the Central Gas Works in Piscatawaytown, across the river in Edison, and a ring-wearing, secret-handshake-knowing Freemason. Before the dentures and all the cigarettes—over a million, at three packs a day for forty years—he had a warm baritone. A union man and an organizer. Former president of the Society for the Preservation and Encouragement of Barber Shop Quartet Singing in America, Laurence Harbor Chapter, he performed in and directed a group called the Harborlite Chorus.

Poppop also had a reputation as an instigator, hailing from a line of Raritan Bay bootleggers and barkeeps. Grew up in a tavern. His mother, Goldie Guscott, owned and tended the ramshackle White Circle Inn in Old Bridge Township, formerly the Cheesequake Hotel, formerly Morgan House, until her death in 1948, three years after Mom was born.

One side of the Guscotts claimed a proud rough-and-tumble Welsh ancestry, a pride divorced from how common folk from Wales are still ill-considered by the English, as expressed by A. A. Gill: *loquacious, dissemblers, immoral liars, stunted, bigoted, dark, ugly, pugnacious little trolls.* The Guscotts are Appalachians who never made it to Appalachia.

The surname locates the Guscotts not in Wales but, historically, across the Bristol Channel, in poor Devonshire, England. There, some desperate transplant of a forbearer—with little to lose in an economically depressed region of England dependent on tin mining, some fishing, and pottery—traded the mucky estuary of the River Severn for that of the Raritan, crossing the Atlantic but never venturing far from its waters.

Could be coincidental, but both Devon and Morgan were renowned in the nineteenth century for their clay-rich soil and the kilns fired along their shores for ages, at opposite ends of the Atlantic, to bake the pots and bricks from mud dug from the mire.

See a clay puller ancestor from Ewenny, Wales, cross the Bristol Channel to settle down in a hamlet called Godescote, little more than a wood near Great Torrington. By day, this forefather is knee- and elbow-deep in the bog, hauling up clay by the armful, all around the mouth of the Severn. Same as his children, then his children's children, and ultimately his children's children's children's children. They all, in turn, want to get out from in between. Don't even care if it's farming farther inland or gone out to sea. Eventually, a recruiting officer comes a-touring through Great Torrington. Calling able-bodied men into Georgie's royal navy. So the ocean it is and war. Maybe aboard one of the hundred-fifty British ships that end up anchored in Raritan Bay in 1777.

These American colonists don't seem so bad. They appear to some young Guscott a lot like poor Welshmen resettled in England. The land, too, looks like Britain. Only the sun's all arse backward, rising over ocean to set over land. And here he is, this Guscott, ordered to sack the estate of one Captain

James Morgan. A home grand enough to have a name, Sand-combe. Raid it, they're commanded.

But what poor homesick Guscott wouldn't give to be back in Devonshire, cutting mud, instead of reluctantly hurling Morgan's prize kiln into the creek the Yanks call Cheesequake. Then the war's over. Royal navy gets bested but good and turns tail. Back in Devon, all Guscott can think of is that Raritan estuary, like a looking glass of the Severn, without its kiln. How, in their new independence, those Yanks'll need a strong hand or two to pull up muck. And wouldn't he like a little of that independence the Yanks fought so gamely for? Even unfairly. Like more than their purses depended on it.

So back across the Atlantic goes Guscott, voluntary this time, mostly. He's signed an indenture for his passage. During those three beholden years, it's not as if he never looks back, regretful. Salty. He does, all the time, each and every day as he stands knee-deep in the muck of the Raritan. Having traded the peasant's yoke for the harness of a promise. Ever off in the distance. Dreamy, dreary. Hard to see a difference, from the mire, between the powdered wig of King George and President Washington's wig.

Come 1850, the Sayre and Fisher Brick Company—stacked over the generational foundations of family terra-cotta works—takes entirely over. Surprise, surprise, the Guscotts are still poor all these generations later. The machine age arrives. Clay from around the Raritan, molded and fired in New Jersey kilns, lays the groundwork for the new revolution, industrial. Powered not by blood but by steam, and sweat, a lot, 'cause boilers are damn hot and need tending, and Guscotts are doing the sweating, now alongside the Irish, Italian, German, Polish, and Jewish poor.

With the arrival of the nation's centennial, as Sayre and Fisher Brick operate most of the factories along the bay, the region gets renamed Sayreville, though still a part of South Amboy. Sayre and Fisher are the leading American manufacturers of enamel brick, building brick, and fire brick. In 1912, those infernal factories spit out sixty-two million bricks a year—all of them far more identical than the best bricks shaped solely by human hand—bricks stamped S&F BCo and laid into the construction of the Empire State Building and the pedestal of the Statue of Liberty.

• • •

By 1941, an eighteen-year-old Harold "Gussy" Guscott bums on the beaches in around the Morgan neighborhood of Sayreville. He's got silt in his blood, Gussy does. And on December 8 of that year, day after Pearl Harbor, he decides he's going to help the British beat back the Germans. He joins the U.S. Navy— only to be shipped in the opposite direction. West across the Pacific. Survives torpedoed boat after boat after boat. Lot of standing around, sicking up on deck. Lot of treading water, fighting not to go down. When he gets home, it's either tend bar, fire brick, or stack it. No more money in booze-running, not now that anyone can buy a drink anytime but Sunday. He doesn't care to spend the rest of his days in a dark tavern destined to burn down. Rather be outside, even when it's cold, wet, and gray. Like in the navy, just no U-boat. No, sir. Home from the sea and the war, back from wrecking all that destruction, surviving some of it, after all that shooting down and blowing up, Gussy decides he's going to raise homes for a change. Do it with the bricks his folk've been shaping, cutting, and firing for ages, and do it on firm damn ground. Then he gets offered a foundations job at the gas works, where he does a little bit of building and maintaining every damn thing imaginable.

• • •

The flesh of Poppop's nose falls flat on his face. His nose does a nosedive on his top lip. Looks more like a mashed thumb than a nose. A welterweight, Poppop boxed in the navy. Poppop couldn't just take a stiff jab. The man took 'em in bunches. He lets me honk the nose.

No cartilage left in there, he tells me, but you bet I gave a whole hell of a lot more'an I got. He chucks an affectionate uppercut to the underside of my chin. His fist smells like a smoked ham hock, but it's nothing but knucklebone. He, too, has been drinking, but Poppop holds his booze tight as a Catholic barkeep constipated on the last night of Lent.

I can tell he's being tender with me. His pinkie doesn't curl fast to his fist. It pokes out, a little loose, more like he's sipping tea than delivering a devastating knockout.

Mom tells stories about Poppop.

How, cleaned up after work, he walks into the American Legion in Laurence Harbor, Post 332, where he and his first wife—Dolly, short for Dorothy, Mom and Gail's mom—spend most evenings. There or, in summer, at Kaiser's Tavern down on Morgan Beach. Mom and Gail, both looking like Shirley Temple, sit on stools sipping their Shirley Temples through paper straws. All sugared up, they put on song-and-dance numbers for the patrons—the men a mix of world war veterans, most of them having played starring roles in the sequel, to hear them tell it—and they hand over fistfuls of pocket change to the darling Guscott gals, sometimes accompanied by their cousin, Donald.

When the girls leave the bar with Donald in tow—to go buy candy down at the small seasonal grocery and delicatessen, Ruane's, run by their great aunt, who might or might not be an actual aunt—Gussy starts stirring the pot. Gets one side of the bar churning one direction. How'bout how, just the other day, Eisenhower refused clemency for that commie-Jew-bastard Rosen-whatsit. Who, if you believe tall "Tail-Gunner" Joe McCarthy, handed the A-bomb over to them Russkies. And did it, they say, right under our own fool noses. Practically down the block. At the old Kepec Chemical plant in Cliffwood. Which is why we got Soviet U-boats parading just offshore day and night.

Poppop then whips up the other side of the bar in the other direction. Arguing they should hang the spying Jew husband, right up the Hudson, there at Sing Sing, all I care. But what about the Jew wife, Ethel? 'Cause come on now. Part of what we was fighting was against all that nonsensical killing of kikes, was it not. Don't care if she's a Jew or no, can't tell me a wife deserves to get the same thing a husband gets. And for what? Hang the wife of that Rosencrantz for marrying a man turned spy? 'Cause if I were a double agent for your Chairman Mao, say, over there in the People's Republic o' China, sure as hell wouldn't clue in innocent ol' Dolly here. You kidding me.

And just before the anti-Semitic stools and misogynist fists were about to fly, Poppop would pay his tab, gather up his gals, and they'd call it a night.

But there Nana goes, flitting between Poppop and Uncle Don, not to be confused with Uncle Donald. She flaps into and out of the kitchen like a Rhode Island Red got caught in the house. She's saying, Oh, Gus, just stop it now, stop riling him all up, whydontcha, there's no need; and, Now, Don, come on, won't you please, have some Christian decency, it's Easter, for heaven sake.

● ● ●

Nana spends all weekend watching Home Shopping Club, buying costume jewelry she shows us but never wears. She offers to sell some to Mom and Gail. Wouldja look at these? You believe these are cubic zirconias? Shine just like diamonds, don't they.

Not wanting us to cause another Venus oil slick, Nana allows a changing of the channel, for a bit. She doesn't want to miss anything. You wouldn't believe the bargains. Show's based right here in Florida, she's saying. St. Petersburg. Bobbi Ray—they call her Bubblin' Bobbi—she says they're going national any day now.

Nana makes me think of Edith, Archie Bunker's wife, on *All in the Family*.

Poppop and Nana have HBO. We're allowed to watch *Braingames*, a show spliced together from flat animated shorts, in the style of the Monty Python cartoons created by Terry Gilliam. The show opens with a rolling disclaimer read by voice actors, accompanied by sound effects:

> *The following program is called BRAINGAMES. It has been known to drive people BANANAS.*
>
> *Innocent viewers often SCREAM at the sight and sound of some of the questions.*
>
> *People with WEAK KNEES or those with a FEAR OF FAILURE are advised to refrain from viewing.*
>
> *Parents should watch ONLY at the discretion of their children. So hold on to your thinking caps and let us begin . . .*

Uncle Don watches with us, because he's not a parent and we don't know what "discretion" is. His eyes drift closed. They flinch open. He doesn't laugh at the cartoon man, shaped like an egg, in a closed room.

The eggman hears knocking. In an Italian accent, the eggman says, again and again, Eh, stoppa dat. Or, Eh, oo is it?

All the knocking opens a crack in one wall. The crack widens. Turns out, the room of the egg-shaped man was an egg.

Dane and I think this hysterical. It's easily the funniest thing we've ever seen. We roll around, it's so funny, smacking the carpet. It's so funny, we start knocking on each other's heads. Eh, stoppa dat. Eh, oo is it? Before you know it, we're punching and kicking. Even our fighting's funny. Until Dane starts crying.

Eh, I say, stoppa dat.

He doesn't, and I get yelled at.

Uncle Don twitches a half-open eye. He doesn't eat dinner with us. He's busy mumbling to himself or to us, we can't tell.

After dinner, we eat more Easter candy while watching Jim Henson's *Fraggle Rock*.

Uncle Don spills his watered-down soda on the sofa but doesn't move to clean it up.

Poppop shouts something at him, and Don rallies to yell back a few curse words. And I know them all.

The yelling and the swearing of the two men grows louder, animated. At first, it's ridiculous.

If they were Muppets, Uncle Don would be Sgt. Floyd Pepper, bassist of Dr. Teeth and the Electric Mayhem, *The Muppet Show* pit band.

Poppop's one of the old cantankerous hecklers, more Statler than Waldorf.

They're starting to get scary but I'm desperate to see how grown men argue and fight for real.

Mom herds my brothers and me into the guestroom. Carrying Shawn, she grabs my arm.

Eh, I say, stoppa dat.

Dane says, Eh, oo is it?

Mom's shushing and corralling us. Jay Dane Shawn, she says, come on. When upset, she runs our names all together like this. Makes me think of an actress I'm in love with, one we've seen in a movie we rented recently, where kids are always breakdancing, *Beat Street*. Not as good as the trilogy of *Breakin'*, *Breakin' 2: Electric Boogaloo*, and *Rappin'*—also known as *Breakdance 3: Electric Boogalee*—but still good.

Again Mom says, Jay Dane Shawn, louder this time, and I dawdle, thinking of Rae Dawn Chong.

• • •

In the bedroom, we're laughing and getting crabby. We're crashing off all the jellybeans and the Peeps. We're three little avalanches of granulated sugar coming down at different rates,

Shawn first, then Dane, with me last, gradual and then all at once. We're more than capable of taking Mom down with us. We peep like chicks. We cry. We whine for our own Fraggles. I want Gobo, Dane likes Boober. Shawn, already asleep, is a cute lump, soft and limp. I poke his cheek. He's a Fraggle with no hand up his puppet.

• • •

I have no memory of what follows. My memory ends even before Mom leaves the room, and it resumes at a Holiday Inn swimming pool, where we spend the following day. Day after Easter. Christ is long risen. There's no Nana, no Poppop. Gail comes and goes, is mostly gone, though she watches us for a time while Mom's gone. Shawn founders in the shallow end, buoyed by swimmies like blood-pressure cuffs. Gail watches distractedly. She's got an egg on her forehead. Blue bruises arc beneath her eyes like an outfielder cutting the glare. She looks like Rocky Raccoon. Dane and I are at the other end of the pool. We set our wet feet on the warning stenciled on the pool deck, NO DIVING. We glance Gail's way and we dive.

When I ask what happened, where's Poppop and Nana, why're we here, I'm told to mind my own business.

But I can't. I don't know why. Minding my own business is like sharing. I'm incapable of it. I sense that giving up some of what I've got is risky. I understand, in my belly, that not knowing what the adults know is not only dangerous, it could get us all killed. So I pester, and when Gail goes, Mom returns, for a changing of the guard.

Mom relents. She tells me the whole story, as if my life depends on it. Over the years, I hear countless retellings, at parties and get-togethers. At birthday dinners when the wine and booze bottles are empty. Years after, I read accounts of the events in archived newspaper articles, written days after the attempted murder. The articles are well-reported and deeply sourced, and where the details don't align with the versions

I've been told, I side with the news as it was reported at the time.

I go so deep into these stories, become so obsessed, that I get lost. I lose myself, and for months at a time. I get depressed, and when I'm depressed, I get panicky. I lose so much of myself, and over such a long stretch, that I come to recall events I could not have lived through. I hear voices I should not hear. What's that say about my recall for what's real? I do my damnedest to square what I've heard and envisioned with the facts relayed in verifiable reports of what happened.

I'm afraid that the voices that I hear are mostly in my head.

• • •

When Mom leaves us sleeping in the guest room, she returns to the living room.

Uncle Don, swaying on his feet, points at Poppop. They stand under the wall-mounted rifle.

Gail and Nana, in the kitchen, aren't cleaning up. They idle, ready to intervene at any moment, spare the men from each other and themselves.

I don't care, says Poppop. You're a crook.

Oh, Gus, Nana says. Please.

What. I don't care who he offed. Don't care who he got to know in Rahway. Or who got to know him. Poppop claps his dentures, points at pointing Don. You owe your mother bail money. You will pay it back. Understand me?

Don doesn't answer. All he says is, Ain't my mother.

Poppop tries again, this time as if he's talking to a yam unearthed only a moment ago. Do you understand me?

Don nods, slowly. Then his head stops bobbing. He tenses, all over. Cords pop in his neck. The ropy muscles of his forearms. "I've had it," he says—from the night of, these are the only lines of dialogue I can document —he says, "I can't take any more."

Don shoves Poppop hard into the kitchen counter.

Poppop thuds and caroms off the countertop. Comes up holding his ribs.

As Poppop gathers his balance, Don reaches for the rifle overhead.

There's a scrum. Gail throws herself into it screaming and grabbing.

Poppop and Mom pound Don.

Nana flaps and cries, Don, Don, what are you doing? It's Easter!

Gail comes out of the scrum with the rifle, saying, Got it! Got it! What should I do with it!

Without waiting for an answer, Gail turns and flings the rifle through the open sliding-glass door. It splashes into the pool.

A stunned interruption of stillness.

Poppop and Mom let go of Don.

The whole family—the awake adults anyway—take a moment to watch the old bolt-action rifle sink to the bottom of the deep end.

Poppop balls his fists but doesn't swing them. He yells, Don, Get out! Get out of my house this instant! He yells so forcefully he needs an attendant hand, near his mouth, to keep from ejecting his false teeth.

Nana's pleading, Oh, Don, please. Please, behave.

Don wades into the kitchen. Yanks open one drawer. Another. Pulls out a long slender triangle that glints in the tube lighting of the drop ceiling. A butcher knife. Ten-inch blade. From a set Nana got for next to nothing.

With the knife leading the way, Don comes around the counter at Poppop.

Don, Poppop says, now, Don. Don't you do anything you'll re—

Don chops the blade straight into Poppop's forehead. From temple to temple, a gash opens. Not like the drawing of a long red line. More like the widening of a big eye. A whale on its side near the surface. Wet and white but bloodless. Then the gash fills red. The red gash overflows. A curtain of bright arterial blood falls all at once into Poppop's eyes. He stumbles back saying, Can't see.

With the knife, Don points to the kitchen phone. Don't just fucking stand there, he shouts. Call for help!

Gail rushes to and picks up the receiver. She dials 9. She dials 1.

Don yanks the receiver out of her hand.

Gail turns to him, saying, I can't ca—

Don punches her square in her forehead.

Gail crashes backward into an end table, the arm of the couch. The TV, muted, has been tuned back to Home Shopping Club. At this moment, anything might be for sale.

Don rips the phone off the kitchen wall. He yanks the cord from the jack.

Sprawled out, Gail's dazed. A swollen egg rises between her eyes.

To Poppop's forehead, Mom applies the compress of an armrest cover.

Nana's there with a handful of dishtowels.

Gail gets up, goes over, takes the towels, and hisses, Jesus, Marge, go in the other room and call the fucking cops.

Nana doesn't budge.

Don makes a lurching move to the back bedroom. There, my brothers and I sleep. We surely dream. Chances are, my brothers and I envision some wacky, reshuffled version of the Easter day's events, as our little brains try to make sense of the doings, performing their wet archival work. I imagine us seeing Fraggles, maybe, making an absolute mess of a tight trailer park. Some Fraggle touching himself indiscreetly. Peeing where he's not supposed to. Reaching out a hand to fondle little slick ladies, ladies that melt, made now of gold, now of chocolate, hollow, and now you're getting smacked. You bad little Fraggle, you. You break. We do, all of us. A crack, a knock on the door, the door of an over-easy neighborhood. Any sunny-side-up street in Venice, Florida. An Italian voice, Eh, oo is it?

• • •

Don's at the closed bedroom door, wafer-thin. A half-inch of air sandwiched between a couple layers of cheap particleboard. The butcher knife—not a drop of blood on it—dangles in his lax hand. He's got the point, poked gently into the door, supporting some of his unsteady weight, a door as secure as a saltine.

Mom rushes after him, tries to stop him from going in, pulls his shoulder.

Don turns. He holds the knife in one hand. He gives it a glance, as if he forgot it was there. Somehow, from some reserve—maybe he hears an echo of Nana's high voice, dyed red like her hair, nearest thing he's had to a mother, our nana, saying, Donny, have some decency, it's Easter, for heaven sake—and, decently, he punches Mom in the stomach with his free hand, his merciful left, doubling her over.

Mom drops to her buckled knees in the hall.

Don stands over her a moment, steady now. Wild the way a little adrenalin always rights the cockeyed world. For a minute anyway. He considers doing to her what's been done to him, countless times. All up in Rahway. He taps the knife on the drywall. He turns and reaches, painstakingly, for the doorknob. He's slipping again, not off his feet but twisting down into himself. Only half-conscious now, if that. He doesn't turn the knob. He holds on tight. Using the knob to keep himself upright.

In the living room, Gail tells Nana, Press Dad's head. Hard.

When Nana does as told, Gail finds another phone and dials 911.

In the other living room, the Florida room, the Venus lamp trickles.

• • •

Don, Mom tries aloud, but no sound comes out of her. No name. She's gasping like a fish pulled from the sea. She sucks air, but only her mouth opens. Air goes no deeper than her tongue.

The second she gets her wind back, still on her knees, she manages to say, Don. When the name comes out breathy, thin, she decides to take a different, more desperate, tack. Not wanting to get punched again. Not wanting to get stabbed. She climbs to her feet. She says, Don, you don't want to go in there. She keeps her voice a whisper. Don, please. She tries to make her voice husky, sexy, but her words catch in her thickened throat. Don. Boys are sleeping. The baby'll start crying. Why don't just you and me—again, a catch—we could go in Dad's room. Just the two of us.

Don's still listing to one side. He nods and loses his balance but stays upright.

Mom can't tell if he means yes or if he means to pass out on his feet.

He slides the long knife in a back pocket of his cutoff shorts. The handle and a couple inches of blade lean out.

Mom reaches a slow hand. Tempted to grab the knife by the handle. She says, Here, let me help. Instead of pulling the knife on him, she takes hold of his hand.

• • •

Mom leads Don stumbling down the hall to the master bedroom. She guides him to the bed. Turns him. Settles him sitting. His nose, his half-open eyes, an inch from her bust. She's breathing heavy, trying not to cry or scream.

Don doesn't seem to notice he's sitting on his knife.

Have to use the ladies, she says. Put in my diaphragm. Be right back.

She shuts the bedroom door behind her.

Rushes to our room. Wakes us. Whisper-hissing, Follow me, fast.

Some sixteen months after her violent rape and assault at Fort Monmouth, the "mugging" where she was repeatedly told she would be killed, would be stabbed to death, Mom scoops up Dane and Shawn, six and soon to be four. I follow. We race to the front door. Nana and Gail help Poppop to his feet and out along with us. Red dish towels pressed to his red forehead.

If Mom balks—at putting her body in harm's way, again, this time to save not just herself but her boys, her father bleeding out on the couch, her battered sister applying pressure to his gash that opened an artery, and her apoplectic stepmother responsible for inviting a murderer of a son/nephew into a house filled with kids for Easter—Mom balks only for a moment.

• • •

Here are some facts, relayed with minimal embellishment. The day after Easter, on 8 April 1985, in South Venice, Florida, a police standoff lasts eight hours. The negotiator asks Mom and Gail, Nana and Poppop, to each take a turn behind the bullhorn, pleading from the driveway for Don to surrender. Poppop sits in a lawn chair. Gauze covers his head like a bathing cap. Eighty stitches closed the gash and sewed up his temporal artery. He'll make a full recovery, but if not for Mom and Gail, Lucky Gussy would've bled out in the living room.

As dusk approaches, a SWAT team prepares to storm the home at 500 Beverly Road. The officers, experts in special weapons and tactics, will enter with their K9 unit, a dog trained to sniff out the suspect, Donald Styles (aka Don Stiles, aka Paul White). Styles may be armed with a butcher's knife and a bolt-action rifle.

• • •

Shortly before 4:30 p.m., not wanting to wait till dark, the SWAT team goes in.

Armed with M16s, they enter through the garage, where Poppop has a little workshop. They follow the lead of the whining dog nearly towing the handler to the back bedroom. The dog barks at the barricaded door.

"*I'll come out,*" Styles shouts from behind the door, "*if you get rid of the dog.*"

The handler radios in for permission, gets the go-ahead, and leads the dog out of the house. Styles is alerted that the dog is off premises.

There's the sound of a dresser sliding out of the way. As the doorknob turns, each member of the SWAT team holds a finger against a stiff combat-weight trigger.

The door opens and Styles surrenders, taken into custody without incident. A knife is found in his back pocket. The rifle is sunk at the bottom of the pool, leaving a rust stain.

• • •

Gail gets home from our extended Easter weekend trip to find her house has been robbed. The robber went in through the bedroom window. He took all her jewelry from her jewelry box, a box that wasn't sitting out, and he stole Maria and her five ferret babies, who'd been left a mountain of dry cat food. Earthstar and Wolfie are fine.

Gail buys bars for all her windows and puts them up herself. She gets a new ferret, Truc, short for Truculent. A few months later, someone breaks in while she's at work and steals that ferret, too.

• • •

Mom drives my brothers and me to Rahway Prison in Avenel, New Jersey. The building has a big dome, like a squat corn silo. I ask if we've been here.

Better hope not.

Did we see a TV show about it maybe? With kids going to jail for a day and getting yelled at?

I don't know.

Scared Staight or something.

Poppop and Nana, Gail and Mom, didn't press attempted murder charges against Donald Styles. But Don got extradited, largely due to the staff reporter working for the *Sarasota Herald-Tribune*, Christopher Clarke, who pieced together the various crimes, some under aliases, that the authorities, before widespread use of computers, didn't or couldn't trace to the single perpetrator, my Uncle Don.

• • •

All-Day Siege at Venice Home Ends Peacefully

Continued from 1A

Jersey only Saturday, but by Sunday evening became abusive after consuming a combination of alcohol and drugs.

One police report said he quarreled with family members over the bail money posted to get him released from a New Jersey jail where he awaited trial for violating the terms of his murder parole, while a department spokesman said the argument had no specific form.

"It was not issue oriented," said Lt. Tom Savage. "He seemed to be disoriented by the alcohol and the drugs."

He said that during the argument Styles ran to the kitchen of the home, grabbed a knife and cut his stepfather across the temple with a single slash.

"I've had it. I can't take it anymore," Styles cried out, according to a police report.

After first telling his relatives to call for help, deputies said Styles struck each of two sisters attempting to summon aid and ripped the telephone from the wall. Styles then ran to neighbors to call for assistance before disappearing into woods near the home.

An extra contingent of Sarasota County deputies searched the area without result Sunday night, and a deputy remained with Margaret Guscott, 61, the parolee's mother, until near 1 a.m. Monday to see if he would return.

Guscott was treated and released at Venice Hospital after 80 stitches closed the wound to his head, deputies said, and then spent the night in a local motel with his two daughters. They were identified on a police report as Gail Guscott, 38, and Sharon Nicorun, 39.

Mrs. Guscott spent the night at the residence alone, they said.

Deputies were called back to the residence shortly after Styles was found asleep in the family car at 7 a.m. Monday, and their arrival set the stage for the day of response.

As Mrs. Guscott fled the home, Styles barricaded himself in a back bedroom of the house, deputies said,

unresponsive to deputies' calls.

Homes near the scene were secured or evacuated of residents, while SWAT team members assembled at a command post three blocks away at the intersection of Beverly and Argyle roads.

Some residents were startled by the sudden turn of events in their pleasant neighborhood.

"He (the suspect) has been out there alone all night and nobody knew what the story was," said a neighbor who wouldn't give his name. "That guy could have broken into any of the houses here."

Others took the SWAT situation in stride, chatting amicably on their front lawns while drinking coffee in the morning, opening their homes to the army of reporters and cameramen who flocked to the scene.

Authorities said Styles was released from prison in New Jersey in June 1984, after serving nearly 13 years for convictions on murder, robbery and breaking and entering charges.

While paroled to Florida, he returned to New Jersey and was arrested in January for illegal possession of a firearm.

He was awaiting trial on that charge of violation of parole when bailed out April 1 by his family for an Easter visit, authorities said.

Officials re-routed school buses away from the scene of the siege. A minister stood by assisting Guscott family members, while a counselor help SWAT members in their attempts to communicate with Styles. SWAT members early Monday morning had electric power and water to the home cut and used bull horns in attempts to contact Styles, with both the parolee's mother and his stepsisters calling out appeals. A portable telephone rang for more than two hours in the garage of the home. Neither attempt drew a response. Authorities theorized it could have been because of the drugs and alcohol the suspect consumed earlier.

Donald Styles

Harold Guscott and his daughter, Gail

STAFF PHOTO/THOMAS BENDER

"Hopefully, he's sleeping it off or whatever," said Savage.

Deputies didn't believe Styles was armed with a gun - but they were not sure. A .22-caliber rifle was either

in the home or possibly tossed onto the lanai or into the swimming pool by Styles.

Ammunition for the weapon was kept in a separate spot, authorities said.

The incident was the fourth SWAT incident in a year, and the third that ended without injury. But authorities said the cautious, drawn out approach used Monday was unrelated to a July 1984 incident in which a suspect died.

"The decisions that are being made here are because of this incident, not past incidents," stressed Savage.] Officials wanted to communicate with the suspect.

"There's no sense in rushing in, we haven't made contact with him," explained Savage. "Standard policy is to wait and try to get the individual to talk with you.

A black helicopter that flew low toward the home was told to go elsewhere.

"Call the airport and tell them to have him get out of here," one officer said in a radio transmission. The same person radioed moments later at 11:15: "If you don't get him out of here, we'll shoot him down. He's mowing everything up."

SWAT commander Captain Ed Palmer said it was the approaching darkness that prompted the decision to send in five team members shortly before 4:30 p.m.

"The risk of his getting by us after dark was greater than, we thought, the risk of us going in before dark," he explained.

He said SWAT team members entered the home through a garage door, coaxed Styles from the back bedroom, then left the home through the front door.

Harold and Margaret Guscott spoke little to reporters through the day, but thanked Sheriff Geoff Monge when he stopped to introduce himself while leaving the scene.

"Sheriff, I want to commend your department. Well done," said Guscott.

"Could we see him ... can I see him," asked Mrs. Guscott a minute later.

Monge told her a visit should be possible today.

Staff writer Judy Huskey contributed to this report.

• • •

At Rahway, Mom, my brothers, and I spend an hour playing in the waiting room. Inside the walls somewhere, Rubin "Hurricane" Carter serves out the final seven months of his wrongful conviction, anticipating a federal district court ruling that claims Carter's prosecution was *predicated upon an appeal to racism rather than reason, and concealment rather than disclosure,* and sets aside the convictions. Three years later, the facility will be renamed East Jersey State Prison, after Rahway locals win a long-standing complaint, but the locals will still call the prison Rahway.

We never see Don that day, and none of us ever see him again. We're told he is not our uncle and is never to be called that. Hear me? We're only here to bring things Nana wants him to have.

When I ask what we brought him, I'm told, A few books. Some snacks, candy bars. A couple cartons of cigarettes, and if you don't behave, I'll be bringing boxes like this to you in here. Hear me?

• • •

Mom has a date. It's serious, and it's not a first date, because she tells us about him. She wants us to meet him. Eventually. Not tonight. Some night soon. When I ask who's gonna watch us, Mom says, Gail's bringing Richie over any minute now.

• • •

One piece of Mom's massive Paul Bunyan furniture set is a standing bar. Its two columns tower as tall as me, and two high swivel stools push in beneath the bar top. Behind the bar Mom performs adult alchemy, and we love to play back there with our action figures, on the shelves in among the technicolor potions.

My favorite backdrop is the Galliano, a yellow liqueur in a skinny skyscraper of a bottle. Or the Vandermint, its windmill on white milk glass, the cap a blue tulip. Mom's favorite is Bailey's. She drinks the Irish cream on special occasions. Sometimes I get a sip. Chartreuse is the color of kryptonite.

Mom kisses me, Dane, and Shawn goodbye. Her hair is huge, her perfume practically a chemical weapon. She tells Richie that dinner is frozen pizza. Already in the oven. It'll be done in ten minutes.

Richie's never watched us at our house before. He seems unsure what to do. We eat in front of the TV. Dane and Shawn want to see *Webster*, but Richie and I want *Knight Rider* so *Knight Rider* it is. But it's a rerun, and we don't have cable like Gail, so Richie calls it boring as shit. Network TV doesn't get good till late, after our bedtime. That's when *Miami Vice* comes on. That show ain't for babies, he says. During commercials, we pillow fight. We wrestle and we box. We get hurt but only a little. The Friday night movie comes on, *Zorro, the Gay Blade*. Richie changes the channel, saying that movie's gay, and then has to mess with the TV antenna, 'cause he's lost the signal. Dane and I go ride our bikes in the basement.

We come back upstairs out of breath. Shawn's drifting off in a corner of the couch.

Richie stands behind the bar. He has a filled glass in front of him. He tells us he's playing bartender. He tells us to call him Lloyd. Lloyd O'Grady. He slaps the bar top, and Shawn flinches awake, and is asleep again straightaway. Richie tells me and Dane to climb the fuck on up. What'll it be, boys. No charge to you.

No charge?

Your money's no good here. Orders from the house. Your house. Yous're the caretakers here. I should know.

He pours us shots of milk he gets from the kitchen fridge. He mixes himself another drink from a few different bottles. Together, the colorful liquids turn brown. He sips and winces and shoots the whole thing to the back of his mouth. He tells us we better not tell our mom what we're doing or else. Got it?

We nod. We got it.

Tired of playing bar, Dane climbs down and joins Shawn on the couch.

Then we're all there. *Miami Vice* is on and it's cool. Richie says this one's the season finale. The cars are rad. The cigarette boats are radder. The clothes are bitchin'. I notice no one wears socks. That's 'cause they're in Florida, dipshit, Richie says, and smacks the back of my head. Some man is saying he's gonna be chopped meat.

The curtains in our living room are pulled closed. Mom usually leaves them open, even at night.

Richie says it's time we should look at magazines. He has a stack out already. He's acting strange. Laughing easy. Swaying some from side to side. He's slurring a little. He's drunk.

When I ask when Mom comes home, he says not till midnight.

He says the magazines were in Mom's room. Found 'em right under her bed. Where everyone always keeps them. He wakes up Dane and Shawn, hands us each a magazine. He tells us we're all in this together. He tells us it's time to pull out our peckers, boys.

I do, Dane does, and our penuses look like ferret babies, but not Shawn's. Shawn's looks a little different. Richie says that's because he's still got a foreskin. Your mom must've forgotten to get him circumcised. What happens after the first kid. Moms get forgetful. Get lazy.

Dane puts his penus away, says he doesn't want to.

Shawn says he needs to pee.

Go pee then, Richie says. Richie has his penus in hand, and as far as I can tell it's circumcised. He tells me to take it.

I don't know what he means. Take it?

In your hand. Go on. It won't bite.

When I don't move, he says, Take it or I punch you.

His penus is warm. It grows in my hand.

Move your hand back and forth. He squints his eyes closed. Faster, he says. Now both hands. Faster, faster. Damn, come on, Jay, you little fat fuck.

When I tell him my arm's getting tired, he tells me, No, not yet.

But I'm slowing. I'm asking if I can stop, please.

Here, he says, open your mouth.

I shake my head no.

No? He punches my shoulder.

Ow, I say, but I don't cry.

Take off your shorts then.

I take off my shorts, somehow easier than opening my mouth. I sit on the couch in my T-shirt and Underoos. I try to focus on the TV, where Tubbs and Crockett take another man, the guy who didn't want to be chopped meat, onto a sailboat. The boat seems to be Crockett's house.

Shawn and Dane sleep in the far corner of the couch. They're little and it's late, way past our bedtime.

Richie tells me turn over, on my stomach. He heaves me up, bends me over the back of one section of couch. I can't see the TV. Naked from the waist down, he climbs on me. He presses his hard penus between the cheeks of my heinie. I've still got on my Underoos. They could be Flash or Spiderman, maybe *Dukes of Hazzard*. I don't remember. Underoos are all that separates me from Richie.

Better not be no Hershey squirts in there, he says. He starts humping me, my butt.

I'm arched in a kind of backbend against the cushioned back of the couch. The weight is crushing. I have a hard time breathing. I sip air.

Richie grunts. Pumps himself against me. Hard, then harder.

I want it over. Mom, I want. I want Mom. Want her to walk in, see what's happening. Make it stop. I wish hard for her to come home. I wish with each hump. Mom, hump. Mom, hump.

She doesn't come. The humping goes on and on. I stop wishing. I think if I stop wishing, maybe the humping will stop, too. It doesn't. I bite the back of the couch.

You like this? You little fat fag. Bet you like this. Don't you. Don't you. Don't you.

I stare at the carpet, into the carpet, the dirty low pile— the humping seems to go on forever—crying now, I start to wish I were dead. With each hump, I want to die. Dead, hump, hump, dead. If I were dead, wouldn't Richie have to stop? If I were dead, wouldn't he get in trouble? But I don't die. The humping doesn't end, ever.

• • •

The humping ends. Richie climbs off me, pushing me hard into the couch cushion. Standing beside me on the couch, he jerks himself off, hard and fast, a wet and cheeky sound. He tells me, Take it. Two hands. I do. Fast, he says. Fast. At's it. Fuck, fuck. Then he's saying he's coming. His semen doesn't shoot. It's an ooze.

He tells me, Touch it. Go on. Now taste it. Maybe I do, I don't know anymore. I don't care. Maybe I had him in my mouth, I can't tell. Who the fuck knows. But if it goes as far as that, it doesn't go any further. I don't think.

He tells me, Get dressed. Quit your crying. Wipe your tears, you little bitch. I didn't hurt you. You know you liked it. Go wash your hands, you little fucking baby. And if you ever tell anyone about this ever, your Mom, Gail, anyone, I will fucking kill you. Then I'll kill them. Understand? Chopped meat, you fucking got me?

When I nod, he hauls off and dead-arms me, punches me surgically. The whole arm goes numb, down to my fingers, tingling for minutes. When I cry hard, heaving on my sobs, Richie goes back to the bar and mixes another drink, pouring from half a dozen jewel-colored bottles. Shimmery behind my tears. All those vivid colors come together to make a drink dark as bilgewater. I don't understand. He sips, winces, and takes another sip.

• • •

Mom gets home. She checks on us. Wakes me, frantic. She says, Richie's so drunk he can't stand. She seems a bit drunk herself. She says, You're okay?

I shrug. I rub my sore arm.

She checks me over. Where'd these bruises on your arms come from?

I shrug, thinking of chopped meat.

Richie do this?

I shake my head no, hard. Dane, I lie.

Dane gave you these bruises.

I shrug.

Did you eat dinner?

I nod.

Okay, she says. She says she's going to run Richie home real fast. She kisses me goodnight, says she loves me. Says she'll be back in a jiffy, and when I start crying, inconsolable, she piles the three of us into the back seat. We're settled. I'm triumphant. Dane and Shawn curl like overcooked noodles, back asleep before the car starts. I sit up, wide awake. None of us wears a seatbelt. Mom fetches and walks Richie to the passenger side. Guiding him down into the front seat, she closes the door. He slumps against the window. He moans and murmurs.

Mom and I laugh at him. We take Ocean Boulevard to Court Street. As we pull up beside the house he shares with his mom, Richie heaves toward the moving target of his knees.

Oh, Richie, God, no, Mom says. Roll the window dow— down.

He throws up a slop of boozy pizza into his own lap.

Oh Jesus, Mom says, jerking the car into park. She gets Richie out. His mom, Jessica, stands on the porch. Mom must've called her. Our mom and Richie's mom help him in-side. Richie's sick, vulnerable, needing the help of two moms. This lends me courage. Makes me believe—for a moment—moms have the power. Two moms. Two moms helping a help-less boy.

When she's back in the car, I say, Mom.

What is it.

She's on edge, I can tell. I'm attuned to her feelings. They tell me more about the world than her words. I can read her feelings like a picture book, but I have a harder time knowing their cause. I worry it's me. It's Richie. I say, Mom?

She doesn't turn. Doesn't adjust the rearview to meet my eyes. I sense resistance, some refusal. There's no way for me to know, and no real way for her to tell me, that it's not me she can't face in that moment. It's the space I occupy.

• • •

FOR OFFICIAL USE ONLY PROP USACIDC DO NOT RELEASE OUTSIDE OR AGENCY

0025-84-CID142-75507

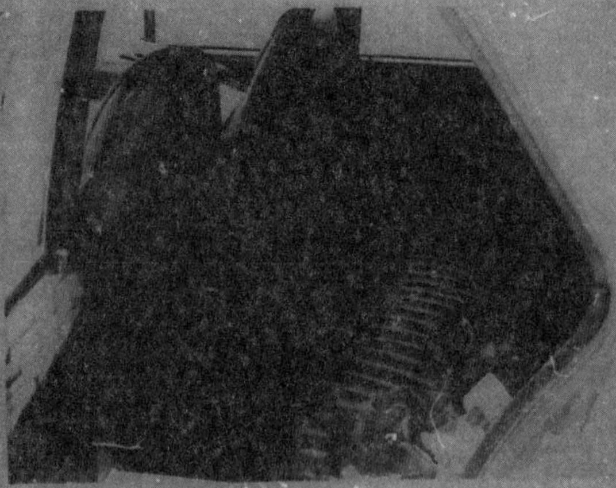

BEST COPY AVAILABLE

Photographs depicting the condition of NICORVO's vehicle, exposed 1225, 24 FEB 84

EXHIBIT 31

FOR OFFICIAL USE ONLY

78

• • •

She cannot make herself look into the back seat. It's dark. It's not cold, not wet, but it is dark. She's upset, I can tell. Tired. It's long after midnight. There's a puke of pepperoni and Pernod spattered all over the passenger door. The car smells like some sort of sour black-licorice jerky.

She turns the ignition. The Valiant cranks and cranks and, as it struggles, Mom pumps the accelerator, giving it gas, but the engine doesn't turn over. Shit, she says. She says, Sorry. She gives it a minute. Resting her forehead on the steering wheel. This happens often enough to the Valiant that I know not to pester. I know, without having to ask, that she doesn't want to flood the carburetor any more than she already has.

While we wait, I say, Mom?

I'm trying, Jay, to get the car started. What is it.

It's smelly.

I know, hon. We'll get Richie's mess cleaned up back home. Just let me get the car started first. She pops open the glovebox. Grabs the regular screwdriver she keeps there for this very occasion. Wait here, she says. Be right back.

I get out of the car.

I thought I told you to wait.

I want to see, I say. I want to be with you.

She kisses my head and raises the hood. She unscrews the wingnut from the cover of the carburetor. Looks like a saucepan and lid. She has me hold the cover. She puts the wingnut in my hand, saying, Whatever you do, don't lose this, okay?

I nod.

She takes up her tool, the long screwdriver.

I can't see!

There's nothing to see. I'm only wedging open the choke with the screwdriver. There. That's it. Okay, back in the car.

Richie's mom comes to the screen door. She shouts through it, Car won't start?

It will in moment, Mom says. She turns to me. Right?

I shrug.

Oh, she says, where's your faith in your mom? She takes the carburetor cover, turns it over. Drop the wingnut in here and then let's try it.

I do as told, and when I open the passenger door, I get walloped by the vomit smell and I slam the door on it.

Please, Mom says, don't wake your brothers.

In the back seat, I lean over the front seatback, my cheek near Mom's. My belly's nervous.

Careful not to wake your brothers. She has the key in the ignition, is about to crank it. Ready?

I nod.

She kisses me on the cheek. For luck, she says, and turns the ignition. The Valiant starts right up. She says, Like magic, and she hops out, saying, Stay here. I mean it. She's back in the car in a moment, replacing the screwdriver, and then she's tucking me back into bed. When she kisses me goodnight, I say, Don't go.

We all need to get some sleep. Been a busy night.

Tell me one more thing.

What.

Anything.

Well, she says. My date was good. I think you guys will like him. He's silly. A little weird, but nice weird.

What's nice weird?

He does karate, for one. That's a little weird. Or something like it. Is kong fu a thing?

It's kung, Mom. Kong's the gorilla.

Kung, she says. Sorry.

What else.

His name's Van.

Like Van Halen?

I guess so.

What kind of car does he drive?

That's your next question?

I shrug.

He drives a van, if you must know.

And his name's Van?

That's right. Now get some sleep.

Weeks later, we meet Van. We get our introduction the day you move in.

Your move takes you minutes and, in that time, everything changes. A blue canvas duffle bag, faded, comes in from your van, where you'll keep your tools. A table saw and a portable generator go to the basement, to be safe. Your van's a beater, what will come to be known, generally, as a kidnapper van, and worse, a rape van, but we're smack in the middle of the 1980s—we're stuck here, together, aren't we, and for all time?—and vans aren't creepy, not yet. The American Age of the Van, though, is on the wane. Having begun with a backfire bang. Circa 1969. That's when Hanna-Barbera introduces the Mystery Machine to a television audience in *Scooby-Doo, Where Are You!* (Why, Scooby, you silly dog, you, you can always be found tootling around in that flower-power ride, along with your shaggy-preppy hodgepodge of a surrogate family, unmasking criminals, solving copycat crimes.) And the Van Age—not that you care—officially comes to a halt in the American suburbs. Lee A. Iacocca starts pumping the brakes, gently but assuredly, in November 1983, when Chrysler launches both the Plymouth Voyager and the Dodge Caravan, and here in 1985, or there, some of us are a couple years into the decade of the minivan. But only if you're middle-class. And we decidedly are not. Neither, apparently, are you, having parked your jalopy van in our drive, in this, the Year of New Coke. Year of Microsoft's Windows 1.0. Year of "We Are the World," with its callback chorus of a response, *We are the children.* Yeah, right. Sure we are. And it's the second year running of *Iacocca*, bestselling autobiography from 1984 to 1985, and your commercials, Lee, are ubiquitous: "*A lot of people think*

America can't cut the mustard anymore, that quality counts for nothing and hard work for even less. And commitment? That went out with the Hula-Hoop. Well, when you've been kicked in the head like we have, you learn pretty quick to put first things first." And can I just tell you, Lee—or should I call you Lido?—how much I loved saying your name aloud when I was a kid. Lee Iacocca. I'd run it all together, Leeiacocca, or I'd space it out a little, Lee Ia Cocca. If I'd had a mantra to meditate on, to levitate on, there in 1985, it would've been your name. Somehow your name meant America to me, then, much more than, say, Amerigo Vespucci, though less than, say, Michael Jackson or Mom, and it also meant nothing to me, your name I mean, so nonsensical, not that it matters to you now, my dear Lee Iacocca.

• • •

You drive one of the Dodge B-series Ram vans, the Trades-man, largely windowless. Looks to've come off the assembly line some years before I did, and it's worse for wear, your old-ass van, but it doesn't have a spot of rust. Gray splotches of Bondo polka-dot the dark green body, filling up rust holes you grinded out, shooting sparks, and slathered over. You haven't yet bothered to sand down the resin filler. Or does that happen later? I have a memory of filling those rust holes with you. So many memories of working beside you, along with you. You were always at work, or at play, and somehow I'm often with you. Helping you. How is that? You were practically a kid. You were weird and we came so quickly to love you. And we were scared of you, but that was part of the love, is part of love, unfortunately, because if love isn't tinged with a measure of fear—at the very least, the fear of losing the loved one—it isn't love at all. And you loved us, of that I have no doubt, but I always felt you loved Dane best. Who could blame you. I couldn't, not now anyway, though I sure did then. But you loved me enough. I wasn't your favorite, fat and surly, and you were hardest on me, which is also an expression of love, if warped. And you were weird. I might've said that already. But it's true. We all were. Weird, that is. And true, we all were. Even when we lied.

• • •

For the first time in my conscious life, we feel like a whole family. I don't like it. We have new rules. We don't eat red meat. Our burgers become turkey. There are locked doors. New noises, coming from Mom, behind the locked doors. And sounds like jumping on the bed, which we're no longer allowed to do. Life feels tighter, cornered. Somehow less free. You're a builder, a maker, a fixer. You like level, straight lines. Right angles. We're losing our distinctions—Jaydaneshawn— learning to be little men. We're bunched up, boxed in. Penned. We're less wild, less rambling. Taught to behave. To be good, which we take to mean: be quiet. Some of our spirit is reined in, pastured. Everything gets squared, justified—can you feel it, even here?—and so we become safer in the outside world, safer from the outside world, but inside, for me at least, there's far more to be afraid of. Our new life together comes to feel like a common miracle—confusing, unbelievable, everyday— and in my fear that this new life of ours is not real, that it can't last, I set out trying to disprove it.

• • •

In May 1985, the Polish pope, John Paul II, visits the Netherlands, and you arrive, Your Holiness, in a bulletproof popemobile, deemed necessary after your assassination attempt, exactly sixty-four years, to the day, from the visitation of Mary, mother of Jesus, to the three shepherd children of Fátima, Portugal, in 1917. In Portuguese, Mary delivers three world-determining secrets to the three children. One of the slugs removed from your intestine in 1981, Most Holy Father, gets set in the crown worn for special occasions by Our

Lady of Fátima, the statue of the Virgin Mary that commemorates the visionary Portuguese site. You even befriend your would-be assassin, call him brother, and you meet his mother. But that, too, is another matter, and comes before, or after. For you are here, Your Holiness, now, in the Netherlands, in 1985—not there, then, in 1981, or in 1917—and you're addressing the International Court of Justice, judicial branch of the United Nations. (This has nothing to do, whatsoever, with the thousands upon thousands of pederast priests in your ranks, oh, Most Holy Father, who, like pervert magi, reach into the swaddling of the Baby Jesus, seeking to confirm His circumcision.) You're at the International Court of Justice to condemn Afrikaner apartheid before the Dutch, denouncing *discrimination—in law or in fact—on the basis of race, origin, color, culture, sex, or religion.* You then, in August, go to Togo, Africa, a nation curiously shaped a little like yourself with your head bowed in your pointed hat. There, you express your wild affinity for animism, the belief that creatures, places, and objects possess a holy essence, perceiving all—rivers and stones, animals and plants and winds, human craftworks, names, and words, spoken and written—as animate, as alive—and you say, my Most Holy Father, there at the source of all that is human, *Nature, exuberant and splendid in this area of forests and lakes, impregnates spirits and hearts with its mystery and orients them spontaneously toward the mystery of He who is the author of life.*

• • •

When we ask what's in the duffle bag, you tell us underwear and your karate belts.

White. Yellow. Orange. Blue. No, you tell us, you've got no black belts. But that's only because you never stay put. No single school or style can contain you. No sensei has stilled you. You're a freelancer, a tramp, a ronin, an errant knight, but really you're an unlicensed general contractor always scrambling for work. A jack-of-all-trades. You've slept many nights in your van, I'm sure. You're a carpenter. Like Jesus, who wasn't really a carpenter. More likely a stoneworker, if He was indeed a laborer at all. You've got a goofy smile, over-bitten. You know, from the nose down, you remind me of the then-mayor of New York City, Ed Koch. But you've got a full head of rambunctious hair, curly, hair you'll soon be shearing in our driveway with a Flowbee electric trimmer duct-taped to your Shop-Vac. You *are* weird. You're boyish. Mom'll tell us you're ten years younger than she is, but that's not true. You're a dozen years younger. She's forty-one when you move in, are moving in, and you're a young twenty-nine. You're almost a kid, and you've never had kids. Although I have some notion of you telling us, over Chinese food, that an old ex after high school, during a breakup, told you if she couldn't have you, she wanted to have your baby. So you got her pregnant and never saw her again. You shrug and tell us, That right there was the '70s. What'd you expect. And if that's so, you have a kid out here somewhere, in the world, who's near my age, but when you move in with us you've never before *raised* kids. Es-pecially not someone else's little punks. That's what you'll call us, punks, and with a silly endearment I can still hear, how you pitch your low voice high and say, Hey, punk.

● ● ●

In the way Mom looks at you, I can tell you're handsome. Manly. I want to say virile, so I say it. Virile. And your move into our half of the duplex on Florence Avenue and Avenel Boulevard takes you a matter of minutes. I know I've said that already. I'm sorry I repeat myself. But having moved as much as I have, I find it shocking, found it shocking even then. A warning. When I ask Mom where's all the rest of your stuff, Mom says, He travels light, and I'm suspicious. Coming up on ten, I'm getting the sense that stuff means stability. You hoist another duffle bag, one word, FARMER, stenciled over-top another, VAN. You drop the bag at my feet. It clanks. Go on, you say, open it on up. The bag nearly overflows with weaponry. You name the weapons as I pull them out. Nunchaku. Sai. Whoa. Training katana. Wow. Tonfa. You demonstrate each weapon. We watch in awe. Dane asks, I try? You say, Of course. You all can. Here. You hand Dane the wood katana with a formal bow. Not a bow like you've just given a performance; a bow like you're about to whup some serious ass, but with respect. Shawn, also bowed to, gets the padded practice nunchaku. I get a bow followed by two black steel sai, each a kind of cross, a cross between a dagger and someone throwing up his hands in confusion. We've never been bowed to before. We've never before been trusted with melee weapons. Wow, I say. Just wow. Wow, Shawn says. He flails the nunchaku and bops himself in the ear. Ow. He laughs. We all do. Careful, Mom says. Please? Dane chops at air. Hee-ya. You take the set of tonfa, two chunky police batons, one for each hand. You twirl and spin them. You thrust and throw kicks over our heads, a kick for each of us. One, two, three, without ever resetting your kicking foot. Your kicks are so fast and forceful, the cuffs of your pants snap. Wow, we all say. Dane says, Gnarly. Okay, Mom says. That's enough a that. I ask, What else can you do? What else? Well, let's see here. Any of you little punks know the Seven Deathblow Strokes? Shawn raises his hand, points to me, and says, He doesn't. Well, I can't show you all seven. Not till you're older. Wouldn't want one of you to go accidentally killing the other two. But I can teach you the one-inch punch. Inside.

• • •

We soon learn you can do splits. You can kick your foot to the face of a man nearly seven feet tall. You don't wear antiperspirant, won't eat dinner cooked in an aluminum pot, won't eat leftovers wrapped in aluminum foil. Aluminum causes Alzheimer's, you say. You refuse to eat steak or hamburgers. You have a mantra, a single word you meditate on—Tell us, tell us, please, we'll give you anything!—and you won't tell us your word, magical, given you by His Holiness, the Maharishi himself, no matter how much we beg. And we beg for years. We grovel long-term. You say you could tell us but then you'd have to deliver to us each, in sequence, the Seven Deathblow Strokes, and you jab a finger, firmly but not without affection, into the pressure point of our jugular notches. One for each of us. We each go down holding our throats. We all choke a little. But it's fun, sort of. Uncomfortable but not mean, not the way Richie hurts us. I don't think. At least not yet. It's pain without malice, mostly. Get up, you tell us. Rise, you say. You say you've seen a ghost, in basic training. In the grenade pit, another enlistee pulled the pin and fumbled his grenade at his own fool feet. Blasted himself to sausage against the blast wall. Days later, everybody in the barracks sees his ghost floating over his top bunk, asleep. Arms crossed. You say you can levitate. You've practiced every martial art there is, and for years. Your favorite is kung fu. You tell us again you can levitate. No, really. But only alone, behind a locked door. You not only believe in reincarnation, you know, for certain, you're a reincarnated Atlantean. Late at night, when it's just you and Mom alone in bed—before Shawn wakes screaming about the black dog in his closet, foaming at the mouth; before Dane wets his bed in the middle of the night and needs a change; before I get up before dawn, every morning, sick to my stomach, dry heaving as I get dressed for school—you tell Mom that Atlanteans visit you. In visions. To guide your decisions. She thinks you're mad. But given the way you've come so quickly to love us, and we to love you, she doesn't care so much, and this is how, and when, she knows she loves you, you crazy Atlantean, you.

• • •

When you move in, do you hang one frame on the wall of Mom's bedroom, the bedroom you both now call yours? In the frame, is there some kind of fancy certificate? Are we told it's a diploma? Arced gently at the top, do we read the words: *Maharishi International University*? Under the name of the college where they taught you to levitate—in Levitation 101?—is there the image of an old bearded man, smiling from out of a gilt circle? Is he more wispy than mystical? Does Dane point and ask, Who's it? Do you say, That, punks, is His Holiness, spiritual guide to the Beatles, sometimes called the giggling guru, Maharishi Mahesh Yogi? Does Shawn say, Like Yogi Bear? Do you instruct us to give His Holiness a little bow? Like this? Do the four of us stand in line? Do we do it giggling? Do you tell us, Get serious, giving me a swift kick in the rump, but only me? Do we press our palms and fingers together the way we do when we pray, and, with your help, do we all tip at the waist? Is that when Dane asks, Now can we finally see the one-inch punch, or what?

• • •

In the living room, you say you need a volunteer. We each raise a hand. Okay, howbout you. I get the sense you don't know my name, and I nod, wondering where Mom is, wondering why you pick me. 'Cause I'm oldest? 'Cause I'm fattest? You position my body in front of the sectional couch. Suddenly nervous, I'm somehow not my body, yet my tummy hurts. I say so. No it doesn't, you say. Mind over matter. I say I change my mind. You say, Doesn't matter. I don't want to. You calm me. You smile with your eyes, with your overbite, a little sharky. You promise me it'll be fine. You won't hurt me. You swear. Not too much. You wink. Just kidding. This won't hurt a bit. Really. You swear on the Maharishi, who fights for only one thing. Know what that one thing is? Global world peace. Here. You hand me a couch cushion, have me hold it to my pounding chest, my chubby stomach, uneasy. You open your hand, like we're going to shake on it. No, you say. We're not shaking hands. Hold the cushion. You touch the tip of your longest finger, your middle, your fuck-you finger, to the cushion held at my chest. Then, you curl your fingers closed into a tight fist without moving your hand. Making a fist makes your knuckles crackle, seems to make your knuckles swell. Your fist, its potential, rests poised one inch from the maroon cushion, the cushion pulled from the sectional couch. Your fist is huge. A fist like a pony keg. It's the rough hand of a man who's worked hard with his hands since he was a boy, a runaway running away from abusive siblings. A hand into which nothing was ever placed gently. Chi power, you say. Ready?

• • •

Without warning I'm dislodged from my body. I'm the age you were then, at that time, twenty-nine. I'm talking seriously about having a child. And, for the life of me, I do not want a boy. A boy will only bring all of this back upon me. A boy will doom me to relive or repeat the past. Those are my options. Relive or repeat. Repeat or relive. If I relive the past—work my way all the way through the worst of it, reconstruct the seemingly endless story of it—maybe I won't repeat it. But that's sure to be living hell, and will take years. If I repeat the past, the reliving of it is foisted upon my son, who, in turn, will be doomed to repeat it. Hell handed down. I sound like the Ancient One, only drunk, and dumb. Blind. Also, deaf. I feel like crippled Dr. Stephen Strange, one-inch-punched into the astral plane. Or onto it. And you, you aren't even you anymore. You're me. I'm the one, after all, doing all the talking for you. For all of you, really. You are all that you are. You are what you are. You are who you are. And you are how I know you. You are how I represent you. And you, all of you, are more than I will ever possibly know.

• • •

I nod and fly back to the far end of the sectional couch. Breathless, clenching my stomach, not painless, I bounce up screaming, Again! Again! Dane and Shawn both shout, No, no, my turn! My turn! Me! Me! Me!

• • •

You are all against me. You all are out to get me. You become indistinguishable. You are all men. You are any boy. I come to see you as a threat. You could be anyone, any man anyway. Or any boy for that matter. You could make a pass at any given moment. All summer long, I see you drive by Gail's house with your girlfriend in her white T-top Trans Am. Sometimes you, Richie, drive, but mostly she drives you. You wave to us from the open top. You steer clear of Gail these days. You go nowhere near Van. I refuse to wave to you. Pretend I don't see you. And it's not that I now hate your fucking-ass guts. I don't know enough to know I should hate you. I don't want to hurt you. I want to avoid you. I only want you to leave me the fuck alone. I have a crush on your girlfriend. She, too, is Italian, beautifully brown-eyed, brown-skinned, brown-haired. Like Alyssa Milano, who will soon involve herself with Corey Haim—reportedly raped as a kid by a nineteen-year-old Charlie Sheen—after the Coreys are cast together in The Lost Boys. And I know why she's with you—you, Richie; not you, Corey. Or you, either, the other Corey, Corey Feldman, never mind Charlie fucking Sheen. You're cool. You're bad. You hurt. But what I don't get is why you did what you fucking did—humping me like a dog, fucking rutting me like a drunk Great Dane in heat, you fucking motherfucker, you—if you have a girlfriend. When I'm a little older, a teenager, confused, and then into my adulthood, more confused, I'll think, You're gay. I'll think, I'm gay. I'll think no one's really fucking gay or we're all really fucking gay. Who cares. I'll think, Well, your girlfriend was Roman fucking Catholic. What'd you expect. Chances are, she wouldn't go all the way with you. And there I was. Next best fucking thing. Am I right or am I right?

• • •

You get busted for breaking and entering. For petty and grand theft. For possession of stolen property. For trespassing. You slip in under the wire as a juvenile offender. You get the stern whiteboy wrist-smack, though some would argue against your whiteness, you eggplant, you. You wop, prone to violence, compelled to steal, a penchant for anarchy, and Roman Catholic at that, you fucking puppet of the pope. When your mom shares this news with Gail, Gail loses it. She accuses you, to your mother, of breaking into her house, repeatedly. It all makes perfect sense. You're her serial home invader. Stealing her jewelry and her Goddamn baby ferrets for Godfuckingsakes. You knew right where everything was. The second and then the third time you broke in, you even got around the bars Gail put up. You must've had a key made. Living like she was in some kind of fucking cage. Jessica says you would never. You're a good kid, just troubled, ever since she and your dad split. When Jessica, a pushover, an alcoholic, puts it to you, you swear all sideways it wasn't you, you would never, in your life, steal someone's pets. Ever. Especially not babies. Who does Gail take you for? Who does she think she is, accusing you? You swear to God. You swear on the Baby Fucking Jesus. You deny the repeated theft like your life depends on it. And who knows. Maybe it does. Because if you admit to stealing from your neighbor, what's next? Acknowledging what you stole from me? But no one believes you. You know that, don't you? Not even your own mom, who, down deep, thinks you're a no-good liar and a thief, and worse, and Jessica's still invited to all Gail and Mom's parties, as long as she doesn't bring you. But then, weeks later, Gail forgives you, a little, even if she can't forget, and you swing by. You don't stay. You drop in just long enough to muss my hair, to punch my shoulder, not hard, given all the adults around, but hard enough to serve as reminder.

Gail tells me about your robbery arrest. She's investigating.
Her forgiveness comes and goes. She's a crime solver. Just
like in *Scooby-Doo*. She's Daphne Blake, only poor, pissed, foulmouthed, and not cartoonish in the fucking least. Okay, she's
nothing like Daphne Blake. She's more like Linda Hamilton
as Sarah Connor in *The Terminator*. Badass, angry, she's ready
to smoke some motherfuckers, man or machine, don't matter.
She asks if I've heard or seen anything that makes me think
you broke into her house and stole from her. I don't think so,
I say. Some magazines maybe? Not talking about magazines.
Talking about my ferrets and my fucking jewelry. No, I say,
and then I ask Gail, in the days that follow, if you were the one
who . . . I can't make myself say it. Not without crying. I try
to swallow the clump in my throat. Who what, Gail says. I say,
Forget it. It's nothing.

• • •

But it's not nothing. And I eventually get up the courage to ask
Gail—when she's not expecting it—if you, Richie, were the
one who mugged Mom. You know, that night. You know what
I'm talking about? The night you woke us up off your couch?
And we all went to the army base? When Mom got all beat
up? Gail, stunned, twists up her face and rears back. What, I
say. I didn't do it. No, she says, of course not. Why would you
even think—Jay, Richie's a delinquent, a crook, he's not a . . .
A what, I say. The man who, the man who did what he did to
your mom, he was Black, and when I say, What do you mean
Black, she says, You know, Black. Like Michael Jackson.

• • •

I mishear things. Or I hear things right but I see them all as-
sfucked. In my mind I mean. I hear wheel*barrel*, not wheel-

barrow, and when Mom gets that brand-new VCR, I ask how we could afford it if sometimes we can't afford gas. She says she got it off the black market. The VCR is slick black plastic. I've heard about this place, the black market, and for years after, I picture a secret store in Highlands, a black house, where kids aren't allowed. Black porch. Red door painted black. Black windows blacked out. The entire interior, too, is black. Black walls, black shelves, and everything on the shelves is black. Black bowls. Jet-black toy jets. Black electronics. Black turtlenecks. You know, the Black Market. Also, and for years, I don't imagine a Black man mugging Mom. In my malformed mind, her attacker is a ninja, clad in all black. Not raceless, simply a blank dressed in black. And not evil either, but bad, surely. An Americanized version of Shô Kosugi—star of *Enter the Ninja*, *Revenge of the Ninja*, and, my favorite at the time, because the cast includes Kosugi's actual sons, Kane and Shane, *Pray for Death*.

• • •

We do more as a family. When you and Mom go on dates, out to Chinese for spicy Kung Pao chicken, your favorite, we three boys go with you. You dare us to taste the whole dried chilies. We don't dare. We love the hot bland tea in little China cups. We fumble our chopsticks. We kiss the paper placemats. Shawn's Year of the Rooster. Dane's Year of the Goat. Mine's the best—Year of the Dragon. I eat goats and roosters for breakfast. Gail often comes, wherever we go, but she stays home when you take us to a Yankees game in the burned-out Bronx. You don't even like baseball, and neither do we. But you're a man and we're boys. In America in 1985, that means bunts and stolen bases. That means sacrifice flies. We pick our way through the outer borough grossly neglected by the final Koch administration. The Bronx is better off than it was in the '70s—it's not on fire—but it's still smoldering. Skirting the edge of New York City is like touring all around the ends of Armageddon. It's amazing. I'm agog. Mom's worried. Rust flakes and garbage fires. Rats big as babies. Homeless throngs. Black husks of burnt cars, one still smoking, barricade the roadsides the nearer we get to Yankee Stadium. Bronx Bombers is right, Mom says. Sheesh. I'm half expecting the Yankees to play not on a baseball diamond but on the set of a *Mad Max* movie. We haven't yet seen the one just out—we'll wait for it to come to video—but we love *Road Warrior*, that barking and biting boy with his razor boomerang, and we know by heart Tina Turner's hit single from the new one, "We Don't Need Another Hero (Thunderdome)," sung a dozen times a day or more—or lip-synced—on MTV while in character as Aunty Entity. We don't understand, then, that part of the reason the song moves us is because we're living its lyrics, and we don't care. We just like the chorus that goes *All the children say*, and then the kids start singing. At a stoplight, two boys not much older than me, a bit darker-skinned, wear do-rags, and it's obvious that they, too, don't need another motherfucking hero. To hell with a hero. What they need's cash. They're robotting. They could pass for machines. A boombox blasts out beats and scratches, a synth sound that sounds familiar. Each boy has a broken-down square of cardboard on his corner. Just like the teenagers down on the boardwalk in Long Branch. What Mom and Gail call breakdancing, known as b-boying to those in the know. I'm imagining Rae Dawn Chong all the sudden, and I'm hiding the hitchhiked crotch of my shorts. Her movie *Beat Street*'s set in the Bronx, I think, and, man, that chase scene, scary, the footrace where Kenny and Ramo dash after Spit, through a subway tunnel—as Eddy Grant's "Electric Avenue" bounces enthusiastically up, like someone's gone and plucked a spring doorstop, Oy!—into a subway station. Spit sprays paint straight in Ramo's face. They grapple on the tracks and fall onto the third rail, fucking fry themselves both to a crisp. The two Bronx-kid breakdancers flank our car, one on each side. Robotically, they spray our windshield with thinned-down Windex and wipe it clean. They're amazing. I want to climb from the car to join them. Maybe make some money. I'm fat but I can do the worm. I'm afraid my worm looks more like a grub but so what. I can wipe a window. The car behind us honks. A couple of empty car-lengths stand between us and the car in front of us. Mom waits, watching you, getting annoyed. She says, Think the car behind us wants us to pull up. I know, you answer, but he's an idiot. In the rearview mirror, you make eye contact with me. Your eyes are scary when I can't see what the rest of your face is doing. In a bad neighborhood, you say—and it's not lost on me, even then, what you mean—you never pull all the way up to the car in front. Do that, you box yourself in. Something happens, you're stuck. When you start driving in a couple years—I'll teach you, I learned to drive back when I was your age, a tractor. Situation like this, always leave yourself a car length or two to slip out quick if need be. Mom's watching you, looking at you, in a weird way, wild but warm. Mom? I say. She turns around and stares into the back bench seat of her old Plymouth Valiant. We three boys sit there, waiting, and she's not seeing us, not answering me. Mom? Can Van teach me to drive? Mom? That's when you produce, from beside the driver seat, a three-foot, inch-wide rod. You say it's a cutoff bō. Half a quarterstaff. Of red oak. Bō's what the Japanese call it, you say. But I call it my nigger-be-quick stick. Mom snaps her face at you. Her look gone from dazed to disgust. Don't you ever, never, use that word, not in front of my boys. Not ever. Hear me? You don't answer. Hear me? You seem to me like an older brother suddenly, like Mom's fourth son, and when I laugh a little at you in trouble, you shake your racist stick at me before tucking it away. There comes a rap at your window wiped squeaky clean. You roll it down, letting in the music. I know it. Herbie Hancock's "Rockit." One of my favorites. I stay up late weekends at Gail's, hoping to see and hear it one last time before falling asleep on her couch. The video is so disturbingly weird that, when I do catch it—again and again; it's in heavy rotation—I spend three-plus minutes in rewound fear and confusion. Those kicking animatronic mannequins, forward and back, dismembered. The dancing pants. A man, with a plaster of Paris head, in bed, bouncing a hand under his covers, masturbotting. The machine baby beating a fist in its empty bowl. And that mechanical stork that claps its beak in a broken window. But here in the Bronx—all busted up before the mean arrival of Rudy Giuliani like a wartime consigliere—the b-boy on the driver's side leans stiffly into the window you've cranked down. He robots his hand through, opens it pneumatically under your chin. You reach by your thigh, and I'm walloped in my gut by a dread for the kid. I'm nearly doubled over. Can see the stick jabbed up, popped straight into the poor kid's throat. But you're only reaching into a pocket. To pull out a ten-dollar bill. Saying, Keep the change. Alright, mister, thanks, and then he and his partner are on to the next car, robotically. When we're through the light, Mom says, Ten dollars for a window wash? You out of your damn mind?

• • •

In the basement, you and I work in the dim light on my science fair project, the ubiquitous volcano. But ours will be special, you tell me. You mean mine, I say. You buy two big cubes of Styrofoam and glue them one on top of the other, gluing those to a four-by-four-foot square of plywood. Then you get to work making a mountain. You shave the Styrofoam into our very own Vesuvius. My Vesuvius. I watch my volcano take shape, desperate to help. When done, the peak stands nearly as tall and me. You bore a wide hole in the top, big enough for a glass vase. Next, you say, comes the clay. Here's where you come in. Mom and I roll out slabs of gray pottery clay you buy in ten-pound blocks. We mold and press the thinned clay skin to the Styrofoam mountain, a mountain so big we run out of clay. When completely covered, days later, the volcano weighs fifty pounds easy. We test the volcano, making eruption after vinegary eruption. I add the drops of orange food coloring. My volcano works beautifully. We build a little forest all around the volcano, and on the day of the science fair, you and Mom heave the volcano into the gymnasium cum cafeteria of Our Lady of Perpetual Help while I march proudly in front of you. When the judges come by, I make my eruption. My volcano takes third place.

• • •

A quick year goes by slow in Jersey. Besides, we're kids. Time to us stretches, like Silly Putty, to a rubbery thread. Only to get balled up tight and bounced around, inside our heads. It's a year of planning and saving, of doubting and second-guessing. Are we really moving? I don't think so. In all this meantime, you're around, mostly. You move out for a few days here or there, but then you're back before we even notice the Maharishi's gone from the bedroom wall. And then even more slow-fast, stop-go time will pass before Mom and Gail have the nerve, and the money, to get serious about a move south to Sarasota. A strange name, if you ask me. Wild and half-crazy but lovely and warm, like Suzanne Somers, a name that sounds to a child's ear like children in the morning, leaning out for . . . Sarasota. A name that evokes one of the year's hit songs by Starship, "Sara"—no Jefferson, lose Airplane—but with bubbles, soda, and how, in the sappy Dust Bowl music video, Sara is Rebecca De Mornay, who hasn't yet played the vindictive widow of a serial molester turned murderous nanny in *The Hand That Rocks the Cradle*. Sarasota. Is no time really a good time for goodbyes?

• • •

As I've said, you're strange and we've quickly come to love you—even though we never say it, we love you, and we wouldn't call it that, love—and we're afraid of you, some. It bears repeating: our fear, founded; and our love, unspoken; and your man's strangeness. I mean, you're a man. That alone is, to us, strange. The closest you get to affection is tugging our toes till they pop. In that little toe-knuckle crack we can almost hear, I love you. That's the best you can do, and it's enough, because Mom is a deluge of love. And you can be mean. You yell. You spank and really kick our butts when we're bad, but so does Mom. You're steelworker solid and strong but you're fast, too, fast as fire in a wicker basket. You stand six feet tall, weigh 212 pounds, and you're not chiseled. You look like you might be a bit soft to the touch. But you're not soft. Not in the least. You let us haul off and punch you hard as we can in your flat gut. Our little punches palsy our hands. Because our boy-fists haven't yet developed the raised knuckles of men, you teach us a swooping, across-the-body wrist strike, an attack in Crane Style. I get so good at the fluid snap of its motion that you'll only let me use it on you before you've eaten, never after. You can jump high, high enough that you hit your head with ease on the eight-foot ceiling. You say you've seen a ghost, how when you were in basic training, in the grenade pit—yeah, yeah—a fellow recruit pulled the pin and fumbled the grenade at his feet. Blasting himself into a hearty red stew. You told us this already, we say. But it was sausage, not stew. Before we knew you, sometimes we'd go to church on Sunday. After you, Sundays are spent watching ninja movies we rent. Ninjas are all the rage. And on Saturdays, after cartoons, it's now the Drive-In Movie double features on WNEW channel 5, the second usually some chop-socky Bruceploitation flick like *Against the Drunken Cats Paw* or *My Young Auntie*. But the absolute awesomest, the one we'd kill to see again, is *Master of the Flying Guillotine*. In it, a blind martial artist *comes from beyond time, from beyond the outer limits of your imagination, he's . . . the master of the flying guillotine, and he's ready to blow your mind.* The flying guillotine is like a big red pincushion attached to a chain. It's really stupid and totally fake and we love it beyond all belief. We throw decapitating pillows on one another's heads. We break a lamp. We say the drunken cat did it. We blame it on young auntie. We forget the cat got eaten by the neighbor's dog. I get a swift bare foot to the toosh. Ow. I watch the rest of the movie standing. Some other master in the movie has these telescopic arms like wacky stilts with hinges for elbows. It's ridiculous and really dumb and the best. When we ask why the blind master of the flying guillotine wears a bib with that Nazi symbol on it—Dane calls it the Swatch stickup; I say I want one of those watches—you say he's blind. He must not know. That or he's just a messy eater.

• • •

You and Mom argue—say, after a picnic party at Gail's, when a friend of theirs comes out of the bathroom with the fly of his jeans stuck down, and when he says he needs help, Mom pries the zipper free with the tine of a fork as Gail snaps photos, photos that get developed and placed in the year's album, 1986, at home on the bookshelf with very few books, and for some reason the photos of the fork and the man's fly in Mom's fingers—the certain reminder, the visual evidence, the accessible shelving of shame—make you even angrier than you were the day of the party, prompting you to move out once more. While you're gone, willing you back home to us, because while you're gone Mom goes out on weekend nights and we need a babysitter, I remove the album page of PG-rated crotch shots under cellophane. I cram the page under the bottom shelf—but you're a good man to have around in a bad situation.

• • •

You move back in and take us go-cart racing. As an unspoken apology, we visit Action Park for my tenth birthday. You tell us half-a-dozen people've died on rides and that's part of the thrill. You encourage me to go on the Tarzan Swing, but I'm fat and can't support my own weight with my hands. I lose my grip straightaway. Belly flop, smack, on the freezing, mountain spring-fed water. The wind's knocked from me, by both the impact and the cold. When I don't drown, you urge me to go off the lower cliff jump, while, at the same time, you take the higher leap, and we do—I do, you do—and I'm giddy afterward but I never want to do it again. Ever. Across the way from Action Park, we go to Motorworld. We shoot tennis balls from air cannons at people caged in tiny go-cart tanks that break down, stranding them under fire. A technician comes out to service the stuck tank, and that's who everyone aims for, but that's just Jersey.

• • •

We downhill ski in the Poconos. Mom and Gail know how, but for you, my brothers, and me, it's a first. We're paused midrun, resting, and you kamikaze toward us, unable to stop, all of us screaming—Pizza! Pizza! Make pizza!—but your skis stay French fries. You idiot, Gail says, after you crash into every last one us, send us flying and sliding down the mountain. You wipe out our whole fucking family. But no one's hurt, not seriously. And afterward, we think it was fun, kind of, but Gail stays really angry. On the way home, we're listening to Gail's battery-powered boombox in the back seat, where she sits with us. Mom's old Plymouth Valiant doesn't have a cassette deck. Doesn't even have an 8-track. All it has is the radio. And we want to hear Gail's new cassette, *Slippery When Wet* by Bon Jovi. Jon's a Jersey boy, born in the same town I was. Gail sets her boombox on the package shelf behind our heads and blasts out "You Give Love a Bad Name," "Livin' on a Prayer," and "Wanted Dead or Alive." At a stoplight, you brake too hard, and when the boombox whacks Gail in the back of the head, hard, she yells, Van, you fucking idiot! Don't you know how to fucking stop! Ever? It's not a real question. And you don't answer. You don't say sorry. You don't say anything. From the reflected strip of your eyes in the rearview mirror—

which should not be confused for your eyes—you seem to me to be smiling.

• • •

We go to the Delaware Water Gap. We hike a trail along a partly frozen bog—ice crusted along the banks—that leads to a falls. I slip on a wet log and plunge to my nose in icy water. You pluck me up and out and cover me in your jacket and I'm convinced you've saved my life.

• • •

We go out on Gail's old motorboat—her shoddy twenty-four-foot inboard—that dies on us every single fucking time without fail. But Mom and Gail are beautiful and wear bikini tops and my brothers and I are the closest thing aboard to men, so there's never a problem getting a tow back to the dock, a dock owned by Harry Hoffman, a middle-aged hippy who looks like Roman Polanski and wears clogs, Harry who hangs out with girls half his age, Harry who'll kill himself in a few years when he's charged with statutory rape. While stranded, the promise of a tow back to shore doesn't stop me, Dane, and Shawn from huddling together in the musty head, whimpering on the cushions over the pump toilet, convinced we're all going to drown. The first time you come with us, you bring a dented red toolbox. On our return, the engine won't turn over. When we start to cry and hide in the cramped cabin, you raise the engine cover, fiddle around greasily for ten minutes with a tool or two at a time, saying to Gail, hand me the this, hand me the that. Gail knows the names of all the tools, and their sizes. When you tell Gail, Try it now, she does. The engine coughs once, twice, and starts up. You tell her, Give it a minute before leaning into the throttle, and Gail calls you a mechanical genius. A real wizard. We can tell she means it, and she welcomes you to pilot us home, saying about the buoys, Remember, it's red, right, returning. From then on, my brothers and I refuse to board *Gail Warnings* unless you come with us with your red toolbox. Red, right, returning is right.

• • •

We learn you are indeed a college graduate, one who owes tens of thousands of dollars in student loans for your four years spent in Fairfield, Iowa, at Maharishi International University, formerly MUM, Maharishi University of Management. You spend hours at a time sitting cross-legged in the middle of the queen-size Paul Bunyan bed you and Mom share—straight back, shoulders dropped, arms slack—meditating transcendentally on the mantra you won't tell us, ever. We venture guesses. Is the word "pizza"? Is the word "word"? Is it "Alabama"? Then you close and lock the door. That's how we know you're levitating.

• • •

Gail sells her little Long Branch sandwich shop, her Wise potato chip route and delivery truck, and buys a majority stake in Cohen's Deli in the Highlands. It's a crazy idea, and Mom thinks it's a stupid, stupid thing to do—getting into business with Al—but she knows she can't stop her little sister from doing anything, ever. Your aunt's stubborn as they come, she says. One morning Mom works for Al, and the next morning she works for Gail, and Gail's like an honest-to-God entrepreneur, only gorgeous. Gail gets a little unorthodox, dares to clean out and liven up the dusty Jewish deli, but she keeps its name, Cohen's. The Cohens don't care what she does as long as she makes her payments. They don't keep kosher anyway, and Al's not someone to be too afraid of. He's not a real gangster, not really. Though there's dark talk of ties to Murder, Inc., the Jewish-Italian mafia outfit, and some of its old dead mobsters, Philip and Irving Cohen, no relation, but it's just local talk, dumb and small, and it's a common name, Cohen, the Jewish Smith. Al, his wife, and his two boys move up the block but still own the building, renting out the apartment atop the store. Gail gets a small-business loan for a commercial fryolator. She deep-fries chicken legs, wings, breasts, thighs, and potato wedges. She concocts a secret recipe for the batter. She clears out a back corner of the deli. Has dollied in a stand-up arcade game she rotates out every month. When we're not at school and the store's slow, which isn't often anymore, Gail pops open the coin-slot door, fingers a metal catch a few times. We get free credits on *Donkey Kong*, *Q*Bert*, *Galaga*. You help her haul in a massive rustic table, blackwashed. Looks vaguely druidic, built for a banquet in a thatch-roof mead hall stacked of stone, a table straight out of some of our favorite movies, *Conan the Barbarian*, *The Beastmaster*, *Red Sonja*, *Krull*. But not *Excalibur*—the table's a rectangle. The kind of table you want to pound with a charred bone while drinking honey-wine from the beloved skull of your slain father-king-uncle. Either that or the transubstantiated blood of the One God. You make an engraved wood sign for the back nook. In black with red letters, the sign reads *Knight's Corner*. The changes attract more customers. The working-class men of the Highlands and surrounds come in a few times a day to chat up the two beautiful blond sisters. One of those men was you, Van. At first, Mom and Gail called you Mister Mustard, because you don't order mayo on your turkey sandwich, like any other normal person in Jersey. That should've been the first warning. Mustard on your turkey. What were they thinking? Business gets so booming that, in little more than a year, Gail sells back her majority share to Al at a good profit. Gail and Al work out a payment plan. Al will pay Gail, monthly over the next five years, a grand total of 90K.

• • •

In March of '87, you take me, Dane, and Shawn to a Jersey civic center for a closed-circuit showing of WrestleMania III projected onto a jumbo screen. We sit on folding chairs in the dark, eat hotdogs, and lose our little minds in the buildup to the main event, where Hulk Hogan defends his title against André the Giant. We listen to Gorilla Monsoon and Jesse Ventura call the matches. We love the Junkyard Dog but it doesn't strike us as strange that Dog, the only Black wrestler, is also the only wrestler in chains. Hulk Hogan's going bald but we don't care. We chant, Viva Tito Santana! We scream Jimmy "Superfly" Snuka. We boo Rowdy Roddy Piper. My favorite is Ricky "the Dragon" Steamboat. Dane likes Macho Man Randy Savage. Shawn roots for Big John Studd. We've never had such a good time without Mom. And something about it is weird, especially at the end. Something's off. Not the way Hulk Hogan pins André the Giant, lifting one of his massive legs, which feels staged. What's wrong is the way you seem defeated. And not by us. Not by the forever battle royal that is raising three little boys. Especially boys that aren't yours. Because we behaved. We tried to be good. We ate our hotdogs. We didn't fight with each other, not that much. We did everything you told us. You didn't lose any of us. We didn't get kidnapped or get run over in the parking lot. No one groped us in the men's room. We peed before we got in the van for the ride home, and didn't pee the van on the ride home, but at home, when all four of us go inside, it feels like goodbye.

• • •

In summer of 1987, third week of July, Mom and Gail fly back to Florida to stay with Poppop and Nana. We don't know this yet, but they're going to close on two houses. One for Gail. One for Mom, my brothers, and me. Meanwhile, you're back—we missed you—to take care of the three of us by yourself for three days. Is this some sort of crucible? Some kind of make-or-break determination you and Mom work out? When Mom and Gail come back from Florida, you will let Mom know whether or not you want to move with us. If Mom and Gail come back, I tell my brothers. Don't be so sure. 'Cause we know, Shawn, you were left on the doorstep by gypsies. No I was not. Oh, yes, and Mom and Gail might've gone off to Aruba, for all we know. Tired of all your crying. Or Alabama, Dane says. It's always Alabama with you, I say. What's with Alabama. You never even been there. He says, So. We all drive to Newark Airport, crying and clinging to Mom and Gail at the terminal drop-off. Shawn whining, Don't go to Alabama. Mom can't answer, she's crying so hard. Gail says, No one's going to Alabama. We're going to Florida, and we'll be back before you know it, now let's go, Shest, fast. In the car, scared, worried, we three boys huddle together like we do in the head of the *Gail Warnings*, certain it's sinking. We are going down. Stop crying, you little punks, and I'll take you to a movie. Want to go see a movie? Want popcorn? Candy? Soda? Shawn's already dry-eyed and yelping, I do, I do! When I ask what movie, you say we'll go see what's playing. At the nearest Newark theatre, you buy four tickets for *RoboCop*, starring Peter Weller. It's R-rated, but that's never stopped us before. It's only violence, you say, it's not like it's sex, and I'm terrorized by the scene in the headquarters of OCP (Omni Consumer Products), the boardroom overlooking a bankrupt Old Detroit of the not-distant future. The double doors of the boardroom whoosh open, and in roars an enforcement droid, ED-209, with machine-gun hands. This petrifies me. What if someone needs help tying a shoe or carrying a baby? Giving and helping and holding have been replaced with guns. This is what's to come. This is where we're headed. The metal monster gets introduced, by the senior president of OCP, as the future of law enforcement. But ED-209 malfunctions. The enforcement droid blows away a young board member. His chest explodes in red mist. Red stew. Red sausage. The body bleeding out red on a white model—built to scale—of New Detroit.

• • •

More haunting, though, are the prime directives RoboCop sees upon bootup—First Directive: *Serve the public trust;* Second Directive: *Protect the innocent;* Third Directive: *Uphold the law;* Fourth Directive: CLASSIFIED—and the spliced scenes, prerecorded, that interrupt the thoughts of RoboCop. How, at the worst possible moments, RoboCop catches glimpses of his former life, his wife, his son—smiling, teasing—glitches that flash before him, staticky smudges distorting the monitor of his mind, making it hard for him to act.

• • •

Day two of Mom gone. My brothers and I haven't yet driven you mad. Or madder. You watch Saturday cartoons with us for a bit. Cats and mice, coyotes and roadrunners, fight to the death, a death that never really kills them. After *Space Ghost* ends, me, Dane, and Shawn go play. I'm RoboCop, I say. Dane's the bad guy. I'm not the bad guy, he says. You're the bad guy. No, you are. You're Clarence Boddicker. I'm RoboCop, and, Shawn, you can be that TV guy. Okay, he says. What TV guy? One who says, *I'd buy that for a dollar!* I give a fake laugh, Ah-haha, and I say it again, *I'd buy that for a dollar!* Ah-haha! I cackle like an evil Benny Hill. Dane tells me to stop that. I don't *like* it, he says. So I say it more, closer, *I'd buy that for a dollar!* and I fake laugh, maniacal, practically in his ear. He tells me, Stop it. Stop it. But I don't, I don't stop it. It's like I can't stop it. It's like being told to stop it only makes me go harder.

• • •

After a lunch of fried bologna sandwiches that you refuse to eat, you tune the station to WNEW channel 5, which we get because you've rigged up some crazy antenna to the roof. We catch the start of the Shaw Brothers' *The Spearman of Death* (aka

The Flag of Iron) produced by Sir Run Run Shaw. When Dane and I start fighting, Tiger Style versus Cobra, and I make Dane cry, you whisk me up in one arm. I laugh, uncomfortably, while you carry me into Mom's bedroom, which is also your bedroom, throw me bouncing onto the Paul Bunyan bed, and shut and lock the door behind you. You tell me I must stop. Stop what? Abusing your brothers. You must stop abusing them, you say. You must. You have no idea how much harm you're causing them. You're not joking. You're spitting mad. And I keep saying, Okay, okay. I promise, please. I won't. That's not good enough. Don't move. You do not leave this room. Okay. I won't. I promise. You go away. I sit there. Scared now. Alone. Wanting Mom. Who has never before been so far away. Not as the crow flies anyway. Though that's not how it feels. I can think of further. You come back a minute later with a length of rope. You tie me, by the wrists, to the footboard of Mom's Paul Bunyan bed. My arms are pulled out straight. Tight. You tell me, This is your punishment. You are bound to this bed till you learn to stop torturing your brothers. You torture them, I torture you. Got it? I nod, and you leave the room. Closing the door behind you. I roll and twist and pull. I laugh. I call out. I cry. When I cry myself out, you come back in. You close the door behind you. That's the scariest part. The shut door. It feels like hours. It's been minutes, maybe half an hour at most. You ask if I'm going to abuse my brothers anymore. I promise I won't, ever again. I swear. My older brothers tortured me, you tell me, and because of it I ran away. I ran away from home when I was fourteen years old and I never went back. I worked on a farm for room and board till I was old enough to join the army. When you saw the ghost, I say. That's right, where I saw the ghost. I went to college. And now here I am. Trying to get you to stop doing what was done to me. Okay, I say. I won' t. I promise. I promise on the Maharishi. You think this is a little funny. You smile and you say, You think this is funny? I shake my head hard. No, I say. I say it firm, trying not to cry, knowing that'll only make you madder. You untie me, saying, Now go watch the rest of the movie, you punk.

• • •

Closing on the two Sarasota houses, both in the 70K dollar range, gets delayed. Gail has no problem. Her credit is amazing. But Van's credit is shit because he doesn't make the payments on his student loans, and when Mom tries to put the mortgage in her name, the bank finds there's a lien on her, a result of unpaid fines and fees owed to the IRS by our deadbeat father.

• • •

Mom tells us an Allied mover is coming, and we need to pack everything up. Why? 'Cause we're moving to Florida! What about the bank? What about the bank? I picture a bank like the Tower of Pisa. I say, The bank that's leaning against you? Mom says, We'll rent-to-own till we can get a mortgage. With help from their friends, Mom and Gail spend marathon days and nights filling cardboard boxes they get from liquor stores. Booze boxes are best for packing, they say. No box is more protective of its contents. The morning of, two movers come and get one look at the giant Paul Bunyan furniture and balk. After some renegotiation, they begin to load the truck, leaving the largest pieces behind, but the bed is coming, and the bar, and the sectional couch. Up inside the base of one section, we find treasures our ferret, Bandit, has been squirreling away for years: a dirty sock, a Boba Fett action figure, a toilet paper tube, a length of ribbon, a chicken bone. When the movers carry out the bookshelves, Mom discovers under them the album page of crumpled photos—her hands working with a fork on a crotch. She shows me the page. Did you do this? I say no. It wasn't me. I swear all sideways it wasn't. I would never, ever, in my life. I swear to God, Mom. I deny the offense like my life depends on it. And who knows. Maybe it does. If not you, she says, then who? Dane, I say, or Shawn. Or Van. I don't know, Mom. I can tell she doesn't believe me, not really. She's angry. At me. Or at Van, and taking it out on me. Mom, I say. Mom? She's not answering. She takes the trouble to find the 1986 album, safe in a vodka box. Shaking her head, she smooths out the page as best she can, replaces it, and re-packs the album. Mom? Mom? Staring into the box, she barks, What is it. When I ask if Van's coming with us to Florida, she says, Jay, get bent.

• • •

Here's the latest plan. We'll drive the three vehicles down to Lorton, Virginia, outside D.C., to catch the Amtrak Auto Train to Sanford, Florida, outside Orlando. And we'll almost miss the train. Mom's car and Gail's car are the last two cars loaded. Van does not board the train with us, nor does his van, but he makes the drive, leading the way. He says goodbye to us at the station, and my brothers and I don't understand what's happening, but we're too excited by travel, and the prospect of the train—a train that carries cars!—to get upset. We have five coach tickets. We will sleep where we sit. Once we're moving, Dane and I go explore. On accident, we find the top tier of a double-decker observation car. Built in 1955, renovated in 1985 and renumbered 9300, the car is the very last of the Great Domes in the entire Amtrak fleet.

• • •

The seating is first come, first served. The Great Dome is a greenhouse and we're plants. That or some sort of low-altitude spaceship. Dane and I tell Mom and Gail, That's where we're sitting, join us if you want, we don't care. We all relocate. It's a little train-length exodus, Mom and Gail schlepping all our stuff, Transformers and Yahtzee and pretzels, while grousing. Then we get to the Great Dome and Mom and Gail both gasp—the on-high view-in-motion is breathtaking. See, we say, we told you! We will spend all our time in the Great Dome, under its arched, smoked glass. Sunny all day, and starry come nightfall. The seventeen-plus hours feel to my brothers and me like months. We might as well be biosphere inhabitants. Living on the train till we reach adulthood. We eat on the train, sleep on the train, pee on the train, but we don't poop. We hold it, squeeze tight our butt cheeks till the feeling goes away. We argue and fight on the train and apologize on the train. We say sorry, like we've been taught, and we mean it, mostly. We keep forgetting where you are, why you're not with us, asking the same question over and over, needing to be retold time and again. You're driving the pets, we're reminded. You're coming with us? Yes, we're told, again. You're meeting us in Florida. I don't believe it. Shawn and Dane clap, Dane especially. The pets? I ask. Where do you think Earthstar is? Gail says. And Wolfie? And KitKat with her six kittens? The two cockatiels, my ferret? Your ferret? I ask, All in Van's van? That's right. Twelve hundred cheeping, meowing, weasel-scented miles, over two days, down to Sarasota. What about all our fish? Gail looks out the window at the wash of green blurring by. She says, Not so sure the fish're gonna make it. But Van's trying. All depends on all the sloshing. Gail asks what's wrong. The fish? I shake my head. She asks, Aren't you happy Van's coming? I shrug. I ask, Are you?

· · ·

All that matters to us is train rhythm. The oh-so-slight blip every second or so where a rail meets a rail—and we cross over those tiny seams. These points of connection have a sound, a whisper-click. You only get a sense of these blips when you're standing. You register the blips in your knees, the space between the knees, where the joints come together. And you don't notice unless you try, hard. Like when taking aim of a rifle, you come to know how drastically your heartbeat bounces your body—blip and then blip—every second or so. And that's how it is, at first—the hair-trigger heartbeat of the Amtrak Auto Train blipping us south to a new life that could very well explode in all our faces. The train feels alive. A gentle danger. In the Great Dome we pretend we're dragon riding. The dragontrain leans into turns. Dragontrain belches out diesel smoke you can taste. Dragontrain roars warnings at every intersection. And we're all alive in the living dragontrain, more alive. Devoured but not dying. Too tough to be digested. Like Jonah. Or just too damn stubborn. But the stubbornness, the resilience, isn't ours. It's the simple, dumb stubbornness of life, of living. Basic survival. It's not special. That's what makes it beautiful. It's everywhere you look. The fight in us is in every living thing. A drive in every cell of every living thing. In every single mitochondrion of every single cell. Each sentenced to survive. You can't help but continue on. Once you get going, you're carried along, as much by momentum as by individual drive. You refuse to fail to thrive. You won't give up, though you may proceed with increasingly less enthusiasm. The hardest part is getting going, and again, once someone or something applies the brake. But what choice do you have, other than suicide, either slow or sudden? There is, for some, the taking of the lives of others. Of ending lives. Or the altering of a life forever, by force. Being change. The illusion of satisfaction that such power brings, being in control—engineer of everything—if only for a moment. This kind of control is exerted easiest on women and kids.

• • •

The weather's good. We watch as the temperate estuaries of the coastal Northeast give way to the hot swamps of the deep South. A tinted sun sets over the Blue Ridge Mountains. When dark on a clear night, the enclosure of the Great Dome becomes a planetarium. The stars stay still as we speed beneath them toward some unknown home. Dane sleeps next to me in the aisle seat, covered up to the shoulders in a little blanket. The chairs don't recline much, and I have a hard time falling asleep, so I tip back my head and open my mouth, thinking I see the Big Dipper, pretending it ladles milk from the Milky Way—too dim to see, too thin these days—into me. Mom, I say, loud on the darkened train car. Mom, I whisper. I think I'm thirsty. Jay, she says, go to sleep.

• • •

When we arrive, Mom's and Gail's cars are, two hours later, the last unloaded from the Auto Train, and then, within days—within moments, it seems—we're the whitetrash family in your Sarasota subdivision you call the county on because of all the crap scattered about the yard. Do the movers simply dump our stuff on the front lawn? No, but they could've. Saved us all some time. Every house is a similar low-slung ranch, stucco-over-block walls stacked quickly and cheaply on slabs in the 1970s, squat, low-roofed homes made to weather hurricanes, all on tight sixth-of-an-acre lots. We ask where's the basement. No basements in Florida. Water table's just under the surface. Our house at 4040 Prescott Street was tiny at first—two-bedroom, one-bath—but the old owners converted the carport into a bedroom. Two more bedrooms and a bathroom got tacked on along the rear. The renovations are out of code—old newspaper insulates the walls behind wafer plywood paneling—and that's why the house is cheap. Five bedrooms re-jiggered into what becomes a leaky 1,700-square-foot hostel. My brothers and I each have our own room. Even before we move in, our house ranks down near the bottom alongside the most run-down, ramshackle houses in Sarasota Springs. We get straight to work running it to further ruin. Basketballs, bicycles, an armory of toy assault rifles. Our messy friends, which we make slowly at first. All the pets pissing, shitting, shedding, and puking. None of us ever willing to clean it up.

The pets arrive safe with you, except for the fish. As a distraction from their mysterious mass death and as an apology—there's some talk they were fed to the cats en route—you arrive with the first Nintendo Entertainment System. You hook it up to an old thirteen-inch color TV in the former carport. The room becomes the Nintendo room and we spend whole years of our lives there, getting our start on *Super Mario Bros.*, *Duck Hunt*, and *Kung Fu*, which you play with us, happily kicking our asses till we get the hang of it, and then the first time you lose, you refuse to play with us anymore.

• • •

We ferry our own Jersey fleas to Florida, or, rather, you do, fleas that, for some perverse reason we all find funny, only feast on you. But a native colony of cockroaches—struggling, surviving on one another's wings and legs in the famine conditions of an empty house for sale—comes included at the closing; German roaches—called "Russian roaches" in Germany—soon thriving in the cozy company of three sloppy boys and the dirty pets, strays forever coming and going and coming; German roaches, nocturnal, who have the run of the place while we sleep, the colony holding nightly convenings under the convention hall of the toaster, in the roach gymnasium behind the fridge, under the leaky auditorium of the kitchen sink, behind and under the range, in the pantry and all the cupboards and drawers, also the walls and ceilings and floors; the German mothers toting behind them their egg sacs—their oothecas!—that, when long and ripe, make them look like they're giving birth to the syphons of clams, egg sacs that drop off and split open, bursting forth thirty to forty little German nymphs, kinda cute, often mistaken for burnt sesame seeds, slow-moving at first, squishable by the dozens, but soon to develop telepathy, knowing before we do when we want to squash them; adolescent and adult German roaches who soon scatter by the hundreds when a light flips on in the

dark, the florescent tubes, fluttering overhead in the drop-
ceiling of the kitchen, adding a strobe effect that multiplies
every roachy movement; the German mothers, now with new
clammy egg sacs—oothecas!—able to lay four hundred eggs
in their one-hundred-day lifespans; their next-generation
nymphs growing through six or so instars, stages between a
molt, before reaching sexual maturity, each molt so risky that
half of all nymphs die before adulthood, eaten midmolt by
the living; winged German roaches that can't really fly but
can glide, which is somehow creepier; German roaches who
emit a smell, growing stronger with their numbers, secreted
collectively or when excited or threatened or simply dead, a
smell that's greasy and nutty, not bad when you don't know
what it is, with a sweet hint of turning fish, the smell of over-
used peanut oil, and you can smell it best in your clean drinking glass; everywhere the feces of German roaches, speck-
ling everything, feces that weep like dried blood got wet; the
German roaches, smallish, that outcompete the colossal pal-
metto bugs big as Matchbox cars and every bit as sturdy; the
deafening talk of the local ER doctors, who monthly remove
roaches from the ears of Sarasotans; German roaches reading
our minds in the dark, sensing our roach-ridden dreams, met-
amorphic and impossible—we both battle the roaches and are
the roaches—roaches tickling our cheeks with their supersen-
sitive antennae, so that we're wide awake to feel them skitter
over our unscreaming faces, our mouths clamped shut for fear
the roaches will dive inside us.

• • •

After enrolling us in the local public schools, getting us on the
free lunch program, the next thing Mom does is take us to the
Sarasota County Sheriff's Office. When we ask why, Mom says,
'Cause you've been three very bad little boys lately. When we
look stricken, she says, Only kidding, jeez. I want to have yous
three fingerprinted. Our father, Tony, come to find, still lives

in Florida, somewhere, wants to visit, someday, and Mom's worried he'll kidnap us. The processing sheriff wears a dark green uniform, has no sideburns, hair shaved high and tight across the top of his ear. While we wipe ink off the pads of our little fingers, the officer shows us a computer console big as a printing press. When I ask if they play video games on it, he says no, but he can plug in anyone's name and search databases across the country to turn up bad guys. He tells me to spell my name, and he types on the keyboard as I do. A moment later, he says, Looks here like there's a Jay Nicorvo in Utah. Wanted for bank robbery. A warrant out for his arrest. He pulls his handcuffs, gleaming silver, from his belt. He slaps one on my wrist, hard. Ow, I say. He says, That you or some other Jay Nicorvo? Do I need to take you in for questioning? I've got the stricken look again—I'm about to cry; my wrist aches—and he releases me with a tiny key, saying, Must be some bizarro Jay Nicorvo.

• • •

You, for your part, set about finding us a martial arts school. One night, you take me to a kung fu class on the second story of a strip mall at the corner of Bee Ridge and McIntosh. The sensei's a slight Englishman in red satin pants that balloon about his legs. High forehead, low part in his thin hair, a frown of a moustache over a thin, lipless mouth. I'm convinced he's Higgins, played by the actor John Hillerman, in *Magnum, P.I.* The class is boring, small, crushing for an out-of-shape fat kid, and repetitive in a way these classes always are. Days later, we eat dinner, Hamburger Helper at the counter, watching your favorite TV show, *Sledge Hammer!* In it, Inspector Hammer talks to his giant revolver. He sleeps and showers with this revolver. We whine. We want to watch Bill Cosby as Cliff Huxtable in *The Cosby Show*, and I want to see Denise, played by Lisa Bonet. I've moved on from Rae Dawn Chong. But I'm told too bad. You get your way, and when *Sledge Ham-*

mer! is over, you drive back to the kung fu school for an evening class. When you leave, we change the channel, to watch *A Different World*, the spinoff starring Lisa Bonet as her Huxtable character at college. You get back late. After we've gone to bed. The next day you tell us we'll never go back to that kung fu school. You say that, after the class, the sensei asked you to stay, for an assessment, and he made a pass at you. When I say, Like with a football, you say, No, he's a homo. You say you had to fight your way out the front door. You say you don't know if it was some sort of test, or what, but boy was that little homo quick.

• • •

Mom gets a job as a clerk at 7-Eleven. She starts at $4 an hour, well above the $3.35 minimum wage, given all her deli experience, and it's full-time with benefits, so my brothers and I are covered when we break our ankles on trampolines, need our countless gashes stitched, suffer mysterious bacterial infections misdiagnosed as spinal meningitis, require reconstructive surgery on a heel bone shattered into five pieces, get into car crash after car crash and, eventually, are hospitalized for psychotic episodes while melting out of our minds on LSD, mescaline, and the local psilocybin mushrooms, which we pluck from cow patties long before dawn in the pastureland east of the interstate. But that comes later.

• • •

You're about to visit—when we ask Mom who you are, who's visiting, and why, she tells us it's you. You're our father, Tony. You want to see us, now that we live only a few hours away. We haven't laid eyes on you since the Christmas of 1981. By the start of school in 1987, you owe Mom tens of thousands of dollars in back child support. You're meeting us at Gail's house, because Mom doesn't want you to know our address. You pull up in a toupee and a soft-top Suzuki Samurai. Mom has us answer the door, and she and Gail stay on the lanai. You ask if we want to go for a ride in your Jeep. I say, That's not a Jeep. You say, I see you know your cars. Why don't you go ask your mom. When we do, she cries. But we go for that ride. You unsnap and roll down the nylon top. I call shotgun, and Dane and Shawn, unbuckled in back, could tumble out at any moment. I get a flash of how, in the heyday of our family, before Shawn was born, we had a midnight blue van with a starry scene airbrushed on one side, and how we'd drive in summers, blasting down the highway with the big sliding side door wide open. One hand always holding fast to the waist of my shorts. You ask how old we are now. I just turned eleven. You say, I missed your birthday. Dane says he's eight. Shawn says he's this many, holding up six fingers. Your life is getting back on track, for the first time since the divorce. You're a pilot in an airshow at Walt Disney World. You fly an ultralight. You know what an ultralight is? It's like a cross between an airplane and a hang glider. Know what a hang glider is? It's like a kite big enough to ride under. That sounds amazing to me but hard to believe. I think maybe you're a liar. There's something unbelievable about all of this. I don't know it then, and it'll be thirty years before I get my hands on a copy, but you're about to self-publish a book of poems titled *Forever Searching*, under a pen name, Rainbow Writer. You also have a new wife, though you don't tell us this, then or ever, and you're born-again.

• • •

You take us through the Burger King drive-through, even though we want Happy Meals at McDonald's. Burger King's here, you say, and you don't know where McDonald's is. With our Whoppers and fries in bags, with our milkshakes sweating in paper cups, you ask if we want to go to the airport. When

I ask, Why, you say, Why do you think? To go somewhere, I say. You ask if we've ever flown on an airplane. I think so, I say. What about you two gentlemen there in the back? Either of you ever flown on an airplane? Yes, Shawn says. Dane says, No you haven't. No, Shawn says. But a train. That's not flying, Dane says. Well, you say, let's take a drive to the airport then. We'll eat our burgers there, you say, and you pat my knee.

●　●　●

The Sarasota-Bradenton Airport is tiny, and not yet international. Takes minutes to drive around the entire airfield, and you park us in front of a chain-link fence at one end of the two crossed runways. When I ask what we're doing here, you say we're watching airplanes land and take off. Why? Because it's fun. We sit and wait and eat. Looks like there's not a whole lot of air traffic today. We finish our burgers. Our milkshakes melt. You tell us about Skyleidoscope. That's the name of the air show you fly in at Disney. You'd invite us to come see it, you say, but the show's been suspended. For an investigation. You tell us the fifteen-minute extravaganza all takes place on and above a lagoon. Then you're quoting to us from the brochure—with some flare. You tell us you did a little acting, with Danny DeVito in around Asbury Park, when you were younger. You two were pals. Though you say you two played more billiards than played roles in plays. But what about Sky-whatsitcalled? Right. Skyleidoscope—*an aerial spectacle that transforms the forty-five-acre World Showcase Lagoon into a colorful fantasyland of purple dragons, exploding gumdrops, and whimsical flying machines.* How's that sound, you say. *The show turns ultralight seaplanes*—that's me—*jet skiers and speedboats, sailboats and airlifted saucers into purple-winged dragons, jet-powered seashells, dragonfly-patrol planes and hang-glider toys.* What do you think, you ask, and when we shrug and chew and suck hard on the thick shakes in our narrow straws, you tell us a friend of yours, Rick Harper, a kid really, all of twenty-seven, one of the other ultralight pilots in the show, well, he died. Died how? A crash. During rehearsals. Just a few weeks ago. One wing of his ultralight just fell right off. Down he went. Puts things in some perspective.

• • •

The sun's hot and there's no shade with the top down. There's not so much as a prop plane in sight. The faded orange windsock sags in the air thick and warm as our shakes. We'll just stay till we see one plane, you say, then we'll go. Don't want your mom to worry. I want Mom, Shawn says. You ask if we know about Bernoulli's principle, how it creates lift under the wing of a plane or a kite or a boomerang even. Mom, Shawn says. Want Mom. Shut up, Dane says. Mommy, Shawn mumbles, and then a jet airplane is screaming in over our heads and landing. Dane says, Can we go now?

• • •

Back at Gail's, we play pool with you on Gail's warped, cheap pool table, while Mom and Gail continue to wait out back on the lanai. You say the surface of Gail's table is more like a put-put green. You try to teach us how to spin some English on the cue ball, but we're too young, and you soon end your visit by giving me, Dane, and Shawn each twenty dollars, and then you hand me a wad of bills, saying, Here. It's not enough but it's something. Do me a favor and give this to your mom for me please. Can I trust you to do that? I nod gravely. It's more money than I've ever seen, maybe three hundred dollars in twenties, and then you say goodbye and go. I don't recall if we hugged or kissed, if you tell us you love us. All I remember, there at the end, is the wad of cash.

• • •

That's the last time Dane or Shawn see you, and I see you once more, a year later, at a child support hearing at the Sarasota County Courthouse. But I don't recognize you, not at first. Mom has kept me out of school, but not Dane and not Shawn. Mom and I get dressed up, like we would for church, if we went to church anymore, which we don't. Mom makes sure I understand what all this is about. Your father doesn't work, you understand me? He doesn't have a job, not on the books anyway. Says he can't afford child support. So we're going to court, and I want him to say this in front of his eldest son. The courtroom's fancy like a church, wood-paneled, high-ceilinged. I watch a bald man enter the courtroom. A flannel short-sleeve shirt, faded blue, unbuttoned to the navel. Hairy chest, dark. A gold chain. Some saint pulling it down into a V. He's wearing cutoff shorts, the denim threads white against his dark thighs. He wears sandals. I've never before seen him without his hair or a hat. He looks Florida homeless. Tan and casual. Like a beach bum. Mom leans in and says, I want you to take a good look at your father. I do as I'm told. I take a good look. It's the last time I ever see him.

• • •

You have towed into the backyard a station wagon that you jack up on cinderblocks, a fixer-upper that you never get round to fixer-upping, a car soon surrounded by the half-dozen derelict lawnmowers you scavenge for parts. All those busted mowers getting lost in the knee-high crabgrass, grass you yell at us to cut, or else, now, dammit. And we do, we mow, now, Dane and I taking turns. One week Dane mows while I weedwhack, then we switch. Shawn, too young for lawn machines, watches, wishing he were bigger so he could use the gas-powered tools of vegetal destruction. All summer long, which in Florida lasts eight months of the year, we can never keep on top of the tropical growth of the grass. Seems to us like the minute we finish with the backyard it's time again to mow the front. And all this in the ninety-degree heat, humid as a jacuzzi in hell. So we procrastinate. We whine and complain and fight over whose turn it isn't. We're the wastrels with Christmas lights dangling from the gutters in August. And the station wagon is the nicest car we ever own, which you bartered for on the cheap given its burned-out engine, that coyly named Plymouth Reliant that only ever hits the road again when finally towed, years later, from our yard for the price of its scrap.

• • •

You're working on a project in the backyard. Weeks pass. The long grass grows longer and you're not on us to mow it. You're distracted. You're staring at a length of plywood. When we ask what you're making, you say, A sign. What are you doing, I say, waiting for it? When you don't laugh, I say, Are you waiting for a sign, get it? You don't get it, or you do but don't think it funny. I'm getting a reputation as a wit, a smartass, and it gets me in trouble, but I can't control myself. When we ask if we can help, you give us tasks. Show me sand the wood, you say. You're Mr. Miyagi, and we're your three little karate kids. Show me paint the sign. You say the sign's gonna be for a man named Karate Kurt. For his dojo. You're making stencils. You're cutting out letters in a wonton font. We show you sand the letters. We show you paint the letters red. You fix them to a white plywood background and frame it all in black. The sign's huge, twice the size of a pool table. It reads *Gulf Coast Karate Dojo*. We help you deliver it. Karate Kurt loves it. We watch you and Karate Kurt hang it over the door of his dojo. Karate Kurt has the sign brightly lit. We marvel every time we drive by. Karate Kurt invites us all out to his ranch east of the interstate. We visit, spend the day feeding his horses, petting their noses, between their nostrils, softer than anything else in the known world. We fish in his pond and we don't catch squat. We eat a picnic lunch. After, he walks us to his outdoor shooting range. At one end is a long table. On it are half a dozen handguns laid out on oilcloth. Some fifty feet away is a stack of hay bales with a paper target tacked to it. We're told we'll each take turns with the guns as Karate Kurt gives us instruction. Kurt is tall and slim with a brush mustache. He seems more cowboy than karate master. He looks like David Carradine not in yellowface. He assigns my brothers and me his smaller caliber pistols, a .22 and a .32. You handle a .38 revolver, and you're talking to it like Inspector Hammer does his .44 Magnum in *Sledge Hammer!* You've given your gun a gender, her. You're saying to the gun, Trust me, I know what I'm doing. Karate Kurt has Mom shoot first, and he says she's a crack shot. I take my turn and squeeze off a half-dozen snappy rounds, each kick of the pistol a thrill. Excited to see if I shot a bull's eye, I dash to the hay bale. I stand before the concentric circles. I poke my finger into a hole torn through the center of the paper and hear a pop. I startle. A burst of sandy dirt at my feet. Behind me, Mom gasps and swears at you. I turn to see wide-eyed Dane and Shawn. Karate Kurt takes the .38 from your hand, saying, Jesus, you could've killed the kid. I return to the table. I think I got a bull's eye, I say. Mom? Mom, what's going on? She glares at you. Dane says to me, You're lucky. Van just almost shot you. When I ask, How, no one has an answer.

• • •

We're not in Florida a year before Al Cohen gets busted for racketeering and tax evasion tied to his loansharking. He's jailed, tried, convicted. Sent off to a federal minimum-security prison for a few years. Forced to declare bankruptcy. Gail loses nearly all of the 90K Al owes her. That's life, she says, and so she earns her license to sell insurance, first for Prudential, then State Farm. She peddles policies for a time, but Florida is one of the last American frontiers. Americans starting over from scratch don't buy insurance, and the retirees have polices riding their pensions. A smart carpetbagger, Gail learns fast that in the South, God is where the money is. She lands a job for Christian Purchasing Network, their mission: *support local churches through the highest quality seating and related church products, all at the very best prices and with trustworthy warranties.* Gail sells benches and chairs. The chairs have names like Jericho, Genesis, Harmony, and Jubilee. Gail becomes a pew-monger. She moves more seats for congregants than anyone else at CPN. As the only woman in a salesforce of a couple dozen, Gail's awarded Salesman of the Year. She's presented a small trophy, in all Christian earnestness, of a plastic man, golden, in a gold suit holding a gold briefcase. Gail also gets a fifty-dollar gift certificate for Outback Steakhouse. She invites us all to dinner. The trophy serves as centerpiece. You meet us there after work. You install faux marble bathrooms and countertops. The surfaces are acrylic polymer swirled with dyes, a knockoff of the Corian manufactured by DuPont. When you cut the acrylic slabs to spec with your circular saw, your work smells like melting plastic. You arrive at the restaurant coated in a fine plastic dust, and before the dinner plates are cleared for dessert, Gail's wiping the blades of the steak knives. Because she only ever carries a wallet, she tucks the knives into Mom's pocketbook. Mom shrugs. I'm outraged. Aunt Gail, that is stealing. Shh, she says. Mom and Gail've had two rounds of gimlets. They're shaking the last drips out of a shared bottle of Chardonnay. Last drop for you, last drop for me. With each drink they've gotten louder, more wicked and witty, and laugh more. I worry about the drive home. I say, What about Richie? Gail says, What about that little prick? Don't you remember how he stole all your stuff? How's what you're doing any different? Shawn says, Yeah, Aunt Gail. Mom says, Yeah, Gail. Dane and you stay out of it. You nurse a St. Pauli Girl. A light drinker, you don't believe in drugs, recreational or medical. You practice mind over meds. We've never seen you drunk. You don't get sick. On weekends, we hardly see Mom and Gail sober. They're fun drunks, mostly. They stay buzzed from Friday night to Sunday afternoon, when they start drying out for the workweek, and somehow we've never known them to be hungover. But on any given weekend, they'll slide into sloppy for an hour here or there, like on this Friday night, when drinks are on the Christian Purchasing Network. Then, the fun becomes endangered. And here they've gone and gotten carried away, into deep water, but they'll soon drift back to shore, where you and I have lost patience with them, while Dane and Shawn are still too young to care, but not too young to notice.

• • •

On the drive home, Mom follows close behind your van. She's swerving. Gail says, Shest, want me to drive? Yeah, Mom, let Gail, I say. Haven't you heard of SADD. Sisters Against Drunk Driving? Mom says, Shut up, Jay. Smartass. I'm fine. Cops aren't out. It's early—sun's still up. I say, That's because you don't stay out after dark. I try not to pay any more attention. During daylight in Florida, it's a lost cause, distinguishing drivers under the influence from drivers with cataracts, drivers with dementia, the herky-jerky drivers with Parkinson's. I'm watching the curb—which I've only recently learned is not called a curve. As we weave toward it, away, and back, my stomach tightens. Nervous, I get upset, and when I'm upset, I don't cry, not anymore, not now that I'm almost a teenager. I argue. I get angry easy. I've learned I can often get my way after Mom's into her weekend drinks. I say, Can we drive home through Newtown? No, Mom says, we're nowhere near Newtown. Please, Mom? What's it with you and Newtown anyway? I like it, I say—a flash of Rae Dawn Chong. Of Lisa Bonet. But that's not all I'm picturing. Since the night of the mugging, Fort Monmouth, 1984, I've grown increasingly aware of Mom's fear of Black men, a fear she hides and fights every chance she gets. Part of my hormonal attraction to the Chongs and Bonets of my televised world is knee-jerk, for sure. I sense resistance, and am drawn to it. The first cassette tape I ever buy is Bob Marley's *Legend*. My second ever music purchase is Ice-T's *Power*. I blast the two tapes in turn—Rasta affection, gangsta anger—at Mom any chance I get. I alternate "One Love/People Get Ready" with "I'm Your Pusher." I want to help her in her struggle, even if I have to force her, so I regularly cajole her to drive through the Black part of Sarasota. Newtown offers perspective, for both of us, and in a few years, on my own, I'll visit the homes of friends there, buy drugs there, and spend weekend nights sleeping there at a girlfriend's place. Newtown is where other Sarasotans live as poor as we do, some far poorer. Come on, Mom. No, she says. Why, Mom—scared? She doesn't answer. Gail, riding shotgun, says one word of warning, a drawn-out Jaaay. I say, What if my best friend was Black, Mom? Mom says, Stop being a little jerk. You've had Black friends your whole entire life. Since you were two and Darryl taught you how to tie your shoes for Godsake. You've got Lamar over our house almost every day. It's never bothered me. So then, Mom, what if I had a Black girlfriend? She doesn't say anything. Mom? What if I brought home a Black girl? She's upset now. And she still doesn't answer. Dane and Shawn sit mum beside me in the back seat. They don't befriend Black kids the way I do, and never will. We're no longer in the Valiant, which died on her. We're in what she could afford, barely, a '76 Oldsmobile Toronado Brougham, old as me, a rusting white exterior with a ratty, plush red interior fading to rust. Sold to her by her mechanic friend, Joe Randle, who's Black. Joe who dotes on her. Joe who comes into her 7-Eleven every day. Joe who attends the parties she throws. Joe who slow dances with her. Joe who swims with us in our pool, his fingernails forever lined in grease. Joe who tosses around the football with us, because one thing Van can't do is throw a spiral. Joe whose son, Herb, was a phenom wide receiver at Sarasota High School, and drafted by the Tampa Bay Buccaneers. Joe who's given her a car before, for next to nothing. Though it didn't last. Joe who Van accuses Mom of having an affair with. Mom paid Joe five hundred dollars for the current car, and it's massive, biggest Olds in the fleet. Mom says it handles like an overloaded barge. Yet it always starts, runs steady. Its old Olds V-8 engine, with a three-speed automatic transmission, gets her eight miles to the gallon, if she's lucky. Halfway down any street block, she must start to make her turn. After a few drinks, her timing's all off. The rear tire rubs the curb. Mom! Oh, shut up, Jay. Shest, maybe I should—Oh, you shut up, too, Gail. You salesman of the year, you. So what if, Mom? What if what. What would you do? About what. She doesn't meet my eyes in the rearview. She's furious, and sobering some. Her driving more serious, if no straighter. My question's preposterous. I'm fat and homely. I'm a bullied twelve-year-old boy, late to the puberty party, with a low-bowl haircut and tits. I've never before kissed anyone but Mom or Gail. What would you do, I say, if I brought home a Black girl? I want to know, Mom, just in case. Jay, she hisses, I would not let her in. How's that. This stuns me. Her, too. Gail gives Mom a look, either surprised or skeptical or both. Mom starts crying. What she's just said goes against everything she and Gail've taught us our whole lives. Mom stopped arguing the point. Started taking a stand against her obnoxious twelve-year-old son. A son, relentless, not about to quit now that he's got her backpedaling, in tears.

• • •

I got introduced to sex at a young age. With gritty porn, hard fucking core. Porn that too often means misogyny but, perversely, can be progressive the lower, and dirtier, you go. Ahead of the American high-cultural curve in its interracial, intragender representations. This while the more respectable softcore stuff, along with the mainstream media, work diligently to maintain a segregationist and heteronorm status quo. Even though my initial exposure to sex was malicious and manipulative—with Richie offering a racially charged, epithet-laced commentary in between wicked punches—the pornography

I saw as a six- and seven-year-old, burned brilliantly into my mind—was subversive. It was straight porn in a queer context. Shown to me by an older boy with his dark cock in his hand, and then in mine, a context spiked with a brand of nonconsensual kiddie S&M—beatings, beratings. The sex acts on display in the pages I was presented were Black men entering white women. Or white men entering Black women. Or Black and white men together bookending one white woman. Or two white men and one Black woman. These staged scenes played into, and against, American taboos. The skin mags I saw in the 1980s had glaring blind spots. Asian women but no Asian men. Two men together always parted by a woman. Three men together likewise separated by a woman, but barely. A trio of cocks of different colors and shapes, though all about the same size, overlarge. Three colossal hard-ons, close quarters. Intimate as fingers in a bowling ball. These foul and alluring magazines are far more inclusive, and far more representative of messy America, than whitewashed, Puritanical, and prissy-ass Playboy, where white women lie naked but not touched, watched but not engaged, the focus on them fuzzy, out of reach, forever unfucked. And all this before the women in porn begin looking like unridable inflatables about to burst at the damn seams. The women in the magazines Richie introduces me to look like Mom and Gail for fucksake. Sure, most of them are big-breasted, but all their breasts are unadulterated. Genuine beauty in the lopsided asymmetry. The women are made individual, made real, by their so-called imperfections. Their bushes are honestly unruly. And now I've gone and got a woody—confusing, disturbing—in the back seat beside my gone-mute brothers, thinking of Mom's pubic hair while trying to break her of her bias. I'm fucking furious, at her, at this fucked-up situation she's got me in—hiding my incestuous erection while arguing against a racist mother who raised me to fight racism. So I do as I was raised. I can't understand her inconsistency, her adult hypocrisy, so common in the grown-ups all around me. I say, What if, Mom, what if I loved her. You still wouldn't let her in? What if I got her pregnant? Howbout that. What'd you do then, Mom? What if I had a half-Black baby? Would you slam the door in the face of your own grandkid? Would you? Huh? Could you? She's crying hard now, weaving the car again. You're not leading us home anymore. You lost us or we lost you. I'm feeling smug, satisfied. I don't care if we crash. Then Gail says, At's enough, Jay, you fucking brat. Because, you know—She looks to Mom, who gives no signal I can see. Your mother, Gail continues, your mother wasn't mugged that night at Fort Monmouth. She turns and faces me, full on. Your mother was raped. By a Black man. You even have any idea what that means? Rape? You little fucking know-it-all, you.

• • •

There is my life before this car ride—I should call it my childhood—and there is my life after. I don't want to be melodramatic and say it was the end of innocence or the death of disillusionment. It wasn't, not by any means. Growing up poor, innocence and disillusionment were in short supply by the time I was twelve. But after that car ride, in the face of the revelation Gail offers, my perspective shifts. The shift is not toward empathy and understanding. I don't gain wisdom. If I were a better boy, kinder, a different boy, gentler, from a different, more generous circumstance, I would've been pulled closer to Mom right away, I think. I hope. I would've worked to console her. Instead, what I fixate on, and for years, what matters most to me is not the new fact of Mom's rape. What lodges in me is her lie. By a shameful leap of kid logic, a lie looms greater than rape. I know now that this happened because the lie was the thing I could understand, to some degree. Whereas the rape—even though I'd been subjected to something similar—was beyond me.

• • •

We get home. I slam straight to my room without saying goodnight. I lie on my bed on my belly. I mash my face in my pillow and scream, loud as I can, I wish I were dead! I scream for half an hour or more. I scream and cry myself out. But I can't sleep. Hours pass. I go to the kitchen, get a glass of milk. The house gone quiet. The roach congress is in session. I plop down in the Nintendo room and insert a cartridge we've rented, *Nobunaga's Ambition*, among the first of the grand strategy video games. These are my favorite, and I'll spend years of my life playing *Romance of the Three Kingdoms* I and II and *Genghis Khan*. They're historically accurate, written and designed in Japan. History told from the perspective of the Far East. These simulations offer a satisfaction I can't get from school. The past made personal. I play *Nobunaga's* for hours, establishing a fiefdom in feudal sixteenth-century Japan, using daimyo Takeda Shingen against the superior Oda Nobunaga. I'm defending Kai prefecture against an invasion when you storm in wearing only underwear. Your tighty-whities shrink your stature. You look ridiculous, except for your grimace. You snap off the TV, pull the plug on the Nintendo, losing me hours of gameplay. Van, I say, what the—You yell how you're trying to sleep. Some of us have work in the morning. Get to bed. Now. You yank me up by the arm, hard. Ow. Give me a hard push-kick in the ass. Ow. I go back to my room, bury my face into my pillow, and scream, but not too loud. No so loud you might come back to send another message. Seems like I fall asleep yelling—I wake up with a start, spluttering, soaking wet. Water in my ear, up my nose. A tsunami crashing on my head, flooding the fief of me, drowning my peasants, wiping out my rice crop. I rub water from my eyes. Can see through the sting that it's morning. Catch a blurred glimpse of you leaving my room. I've been deluged. My bed drenched. The carpet spongy. You didn't toss a cup, splash a bowl of water on me. You dumped on me a brimful five-gallon bucket. I wade into the kitchen. I stand there dripping, waiting for Mom to notice me. She flips pancakes on the griddle. Morning, Hun, she

says. She goes to give me a kiss. She flinches. Why are you—
Why, because Van just woke me by dumping cold water on me.
In bed. My mattress is now soaked. It'll take days to dry. And
I have no idea why.

• • •

The more I imagine it—and I imagine it more than I should—
the more I feel for Mom and her rape. But it's slow going. Because I can't, at the time, forgive her for her lie. Her lie has
warped whole years of my life, a full quarter of it. There she
was, telling me to be honest, to be truthful, and all the while
she's been lying. All through my adolescence, I can't let it go.
I want to know what else she's been concealing. What else
she's been distorting. Her lie causes me to call everything into
question. Every fucking thing. Is my father really my father?
Is he father to both my brothers? Has she omitted crucial as-
pects of their divorce? The worst of it is this: her initial lie
makes me doubt the eventual truth. I call her rape into question. I want specifics. I want the terrible particulars. The devil
is there, in the details, but God is found in fact.

• • •

You are not love. It's really that simple. I don't care what John
says, in his first letter, which begins, My little children, these
things write I unto you, that ye sin not. We children do sin. We do
wrong. I can attest to that. And then, in Your name, and with
Your authority, John goes on: Beloved, believe not every spirit, but
try the spirits whether they are of God: because many false prophets are
gone out into the world. This is true enough. And John is also true
when he writes that love is of You. But he goes too far, becomes false, when he writes, in this letter of his addressed to
little children, that You are love. You are not. You are not love.
And, I fear, you simply are not. You aren't. You don't exist. But
if You do, You, God, are truth. Not love. Above and beyond all

else. How do I know? Because truth is possible without love. This means You are possible without love. But without truth, there can be no love. And without truth, You can't be possible. Love is wholly dependent on truth, as are You. If a love is built on a lie—even if that lie is You—then that love is not real, even if it offers consolation. Even if it inspires goodness. Even if it keeps us from despair. Even if it helps us from hating our brother. The consolation is real. The goodness is real. The pull from despair is real. The help against hate is real. But none of this makes You real. No more real than a good story, anyway, or a revolutionary idea. This is the shadow of a doubt, dear God, ever-present, the doubt that throws a valley of shade on all existence. A doubt that diminishes all fact to a lesser degree. Because by taking the measure of a fact, we change it. Acknowledging a fact alters that fact by the very act of acknowledgment. But facts can prove—beyond a reasonable doubt if never beyond Your shadow—that the rape of Mom is real, even if You, by God, are not.

• • •

At twelve years old, I can't form the right questions. I can't start the conversation. I don't have enough information. I don't know where to begin. Despite my early exposure to sex and to sexual abuse—and maybe even because of it—I don't know the real difference between rape and sex. I think back to the night of Mom's rape, ground wet, dark. I think back to the nights of my molestation. I think about the drawn curtains in our living room, about the dark hedgerow outside the window onto Avenel Boulevard. How, in daylight I'd seen a larger praying mantis, the female, devouring a smaller man mantis. How she starts eating at his back end and works her way up him. I know they're lovers. Half-eaten, he's no longer praying. He waves his arms. When all that's left is his head, I turn away and go tell Mom what I've witnessed. She explains the context. I don't really know, in 1988, where rape starts and sex ends. Seems like not even 1988 knows. Even the laws, then, are radically different. It'll be five years before all fifty states have criminalized marital rape, and still, to this day, a dozen states have separate statutes for rape and spousal rape. In 1988, I do know rape is one of the worst things a person—usually a man but not always, especially not if you're a mantis—can do, but I can't fathom it. Not really. It doesn't occur to me that what Richie did to me approaches rape. That it was rape lite. Mom's lie, though, that I can grasp. I hold fast to it, and for years. A gross distortion. A manipulation. A violation. I want to go back to the moments after that car ride. I am going back to the moments after that car ride. I pull aside that twelve-year-old version of me. I say, Hey, you fat little fuck. Maybe try to think of it this way. What rape is to sex, a lie is to truth. While you're at it, be better to your mom. She's doing the best she can. And given the shit circumstances, her efforts are heroic.

• • •

I do not look for you everywhere, but I find you on TV and in movies. I try to memorize your schedule in the TV Guide. You're Mr. Brady, Fred Sanford, RoboCop, Cliff Huxtable, Merlin, Optimus Prime. The list goes on. Lee Iacocca, Oda Nobunaga, the Maharishi, Pope John Paul II, God, Mom. Yet the you I most want you to be, on TV at least, is Roc Emerson, the Baltimore garbage man, played by Charles S. Dutton, in the sitcom Roc. You, Roc, are all the things I hope for in a dad. You're flawed but good, and I'm not sure how it got to be so, but as I sit there watching your show, I come to love your character and then you, as an actor. I'm floored by season two, where every episode airs live. You're not only one of the best actors on TV, you may be the best man I know, and it does occur to me you're Black, I do see race, and all too well, but it couldn't matter to me less. Or maybe what matters to me is that you are of a different race. Or that you're the same race as

Mom's rapist. I find out that you killed a man in a fight when you were seventeen, and spent nine years in prison. There, you read a play in solitary confinement, a play that changes your life, *Day of Absence* by Douglas Turner Ward, a play cast by Blacks in whiteface. All this only makes me, ridiculously, want you all the more for my father.

• • •

I come home from school. Go into the bedroom you share with Mom. I'm searching for the *TV Guide*, usually by her bedside, where she works on the crossword each night. Not there. I look in the bathroom. There, I find you. You sit on the toilet. The toilet looks tiny under you, precarious. You're like a grown-ass man riding a white tricycle. A ghost trike. I laugh a little. You look vulnerable, with your penus, nowhere to be seen, tucked between your legs, dangling down presumably in the bowl. I say, Oops, sorry. Back out, closing the door. Then, only after, I register the look on your face—hatred. And not just hatred for the kid I am, but hatred for the man you see me becoming. I go to my room. I don't close the door. I sit on my bed. I wait. How long does it take to finish a shit? To wipe an ass? Two minutes later, I hear you coming. You're the sound of my terror. Not loud. That's the most terrifying part. You move from one end of the house to the other with predatory force and determination. I have just enough time—to picture the alien in *Alien* scrambling through the airshafts of the Nostromo, and to whisper, Ah, fuck, as you barrel round the hall corner and come through my doorway midflight. Now that you're here, having arrived, you're less of a threat. But I'm sensing there's nothing playful about your flying leap in my direction, and it's not staged, yet I can't help feel it's partly for show. A put-on, because if you went all out, I would be dead in a moment. I am no match for you, and we both know, no matter how big and strong I grow, finally thinning out, no matter how many years of judo I take and how many medals

I win, among them a gold in my weight class at the Sunshine State Games, I will never be your match. You're still hanging midflight—I'm stalling, forgive me—you're Jimmy "Superfly" Snuka off the top turnbuckle. I'm little more than a kid in the audience caught up in the scuffle. And I find it funny, ridiculous even, until your body slams, wham, into mine. Your diving tackle is so fast, so powerful, that, when you land on me, our weight snaps the two far-side bed legs. We're dumped into the wall, onto the floor. You on me. You're yelling. You rough me up in a close-quarters, ground-and-pound kind of way. I'm on my stomach; you're on my back. As it's ongoing, I know you're pulling punches. After a minute of what in judo we call mat work—grappling on hands and knees—a minute where I don't fight back but simply cover up, a domination minute, you push off me. You stand, say something I can't recall, or don't hear, and you leave. I don't dare move. I stay curled, fetal, not crying yet, stunned. In shock. Trying to understand how catching you midshit made you go berserk. I hear you coming back. Again, a flying leap. This time sliding down the cockeyed bed and onto me. Another go at ground-and-pound. My fists tight against my ears, like I've been taught. I don't want cauliflower ears, like the serious judokas I've lost to. I'm not that serious, but I have spunk. I make out your words this round. Something about me stealing from you. I manage to say the TV Guide's not even yours. This makes you madder. You drop elbows and forearms on me. I know you're landing purposeful blows on my soft spots, so you don't open me up, so the evidence is minimal. You push hard off me and up. You're gone again. Before I have time to make a little more sense, you're back. On me once more. Your weight familiar. Pressing. A burden, mine. Your body crushing and suffocating, but not physically. Or not merely physical. You push my head, my face. You rub my face hard with your rough open hand. You scream into my ear, Liar! Thief! You say, You've been stealing from me for years! And I'm sick of it! I've had it! And then you're up and off me and gone again. And again you're back. I'm keep-

ing count. This is your fifth return for more. Or sixth. I'm losing count. I'm crying now. Hard. I'm losing more than the
count. I'm worried this will never end. You will forever and
always be returning to throw all of your weight on top of me
tucked fetal beside my busted bed. You're gone again. Again,
I wait. When you don't return, I'm convinced it's only a matter of time. More minutes pass. I decide I'm not going to give
you another chance to kill me. I crawl from beside my bed. I
open the door of my closet, tuck in to one corner on top of
the mess, crying, and close the door behind me. I'm there for
an hour, easy. You don't come back. I decide I will stay where
I am, curled crying in the closet, till Mom comes home. If she
finds me like this, she will throw you out for good, I'm certain.
If I can just be patient, play my role as victim a little longer,
you will be gone from us forever and we can have some peace.
We can breathe. Get on with our lives. I spend another restless
half-hour in the closet before I can't take any more. I get up. I
go tentatively into the kitchen, look out the living room window. Your van's gone. You're gone, but not for good. Not yet,
even though when Mom finally comes home, sees my broken
bed, hears what I have to tell her, you are in some deep fucking
shit. I've got rug burn and a bruise or two, but I'm not bloody.
Inside, though, I've been broken. Or rebroken. I say, It's either
him or me, Mom. If he doesn't leave for good, I'm gone. I will
run away. I swear. I will go live with Gail. 'Cause she under-
stands, after you dragged her ass kicking and screaming out
of our house not but a month before. But this, this still isn't
the beginning of the end. Not really. Our scuffle prompts one
of your weekend expulsions, one where you take with you the
thirty-two-inch TV you bought used for my brothers and me
as a Christmas gift. When you move back in, returning the
TV, you make a kind of peace offering. And that's what brings
about the beginning of the end. The peace offering less than all
the abuse. Your big revelation is what ultimately does you in.
You decide to demonstrate for us—Mom, Gail, Dane, Shawn,
me—your powers of levitation.

The thing is, I have been stealing from you. That's the hardest part to reconcile. I come to believe I deserve what I got, what punishment you served up, I just didn't deserve it in that moment. All summer long, I'd been taking quarters from you. When Mom drops us off at the Boys and Girls Club of Sarasota, she gives us each seventy-five cents to last us from 7 a.m. till 4 p.m. We've got the math worked out. We get to play one video game every three hours. I blow my quarters in the first few minutes. Dane spaces his out, dropping one quarter exactly every three hours. Shawn either loses his quarters, or gives them away, or someone steals them from him, or I con them out of him. For the remaining eight and a half hours that we're not playing video games, we play four square. That is, unless I've stolen a few extra quarters from you. I fight a lot with other kids who call me a girl. Kids give me purple nurples. I've still got a lot of nipple to grab on to. They twist and pinch my tit till it bruises, and I haul off and hit them, using the force of my hips by torquing quick at the waist. I hit them hard like I've been taught, and they leave me the fuck alone.

• • •

Years of wearing you down did nothing to open you up about your mantra. But as a kind of consolation to all the desperate begging becoming disbelief, becoming, the older we get, barely disguised mockery, you line us up in the dining area we never use. You clear aside some ten feet of space on the carpet. Dane says, What's this, your runway? You don't answer. No, I say, that's the levitation launchpad. We're wild with excitement. Shawn jumps up and down. Dane is shrugging in disbelief. Gail and Mom watch but seem uneasy. We've lived in anticipation of this moment for years. Okay, you say. You sit cross-legged on the stained carpet. You close your eyes. You perch your hands on your knees. You om. Shawn says, Why's he humming? Dane gets down low, puts his cheek to the carpet. What're you doing, I ask. Dane says, Still on the ground. Hasn't achieved liftoff. Your oming gets louder. You grin. I grow a little scared. If you do levitate, everything changes. My world turns downside-up. Aliens exist. Ghosts are real. Atlantis gets found. God dies. Or God is proved. I don't know which. If you don't levitate, everything also changes. Because then, we know you're a liar, or worse. You are fucking batshit ass crazy. As you om, I come to realize there's only one way your claims of levitation can function: as a claim. A promise. As faith. God works, and doesn't work, in the same mysterious way. Existing somewhere between fact and fiction. Never one nor the other. The moment levitation is either proved or disproved, faith is strangled. Becomes useless. The end of both belief and disbelief. This is lose-lose. Your oming now is so loud it's unbearable. And then, from your lotus position, sitting still like a curly haired Buddha, you contract your posture, coiling down into yourself, forcing your heart into your lap. Your hands cup your knees and—keeping your seated, cross-legged posture all the while—you bound some six or so feet across the room. I look at Dane. He shrugs. Mom and Gail wait a moment. When I see that they've decided the demonstration's over, when they shake their heads, when they go back to their drinks, I laugh. I don't know what else to do. It's awkward. It is finished. The sitting leap would've been an astounding feat of flexibility and strength if, for years, it hadn't been called levitation. Whenever you closed yourself behind the locked bedroom door, got centered on the creaky bedsprings, and omed, I imagined you hovering a foot off the mattress, casting a golden light against the walls from some source deep within yourself. Shining your heartlight into the world to help the Maharishi bring about global world-ass peace. But no. What we just witnessed wasn't hovering. It was not floating. Looked more like desperation. The sad hop of a paraplegic kangaroo. I'm not sure if this now proves that God is dead or alive, but I'm outraged. That it? I say. That was levitating? You stand up, flushed. Smiling, you are glowing, some. The glow isn't mystical. Seems a little embarrassed. Weirdly, you also seem proud of yourself, the distance you cleared. Shawn says, You see that! He jumped like a frog! Yeah, I say, ribbit. Dane says, That's not levitating. No, I say, it's not. Dane says, That's lying. Mom and Gail are laughing now. Mom says, Dane, go play. They've got their next round of screwdrivers mixed with orange-juice concentrate and the cheapest vodka money can buy. The brand name is Vodka. Nice one, Van, Gail says. You jerk. She turns and heads outside, and that feeling you're feeling, in that moment, the spiral draw downward, like water sucking round down the drain, that's the feeling of losing regard, gradually at first and then all at once. Gone. It's the moment a reputation is ruined. If there's any saving face, it'll take years of work—years of piecing together a new narrative, one not founded on a lie, or a secret—and you're not up to it. At least not with us, you're not. You're getting the uneasy, inchoate sense something's changed, is changing. You feel the paradigm shift as we each turn our backs on you and go about our business, as if nothing happened. And that's the problem. You made nothing happen. What's saddest is not that, after years of withholding from us, we no longer believe you from this point forward. What's saddest isn't even that, from here on out, we will care less what you withhold because, chances are, it's hollow. What is saddest, what's devastating, is that you still so obviously believe your version of the truth. You think you're sane and we're all crazy. What a lonely feeling that must be for you. You're convinced hopping is levitating. What the Maharishi calls levitating, calls yogic flying, is nothing more than toad yoga. Your Maharishi is a con man. You've put on a demonstration; you've demonstrated delusion. You performed a public execution of the truth. So what if truth gets a bad rap these days. The truth gets distorted, can be seen, by the cynical, as nothing more than a tool of oppression employed by those in power. But the truth is the best we have. The truth is the best we can do. The truth is the best the world has to offer—for the powerful and the powerless both—because the truth is the closest we ever get to the world. We never *are* the world. The song is wrong. We are only ever in the world. A miniscule part of it. Observing. Trying to make sense of it. We're always working toward the hard truth, when we try hard. We never achieve the whole truth, nothing but the truth. And the moment we stop working toward truth, that's when the center no longer holds. That's how the world ends. Not with a bang. Not with a whimper. The world ends with a liar. And maybe because none of us can trust you anymore, you leave for work on Monday morning and start an affair. With a woman who's contracted you to install her faux marble bathroom. You need to give some credence to the palpable lack of belief in our house. You need to make our newfound mistrust into something real, make our disbelief about something you can do rather than something you can't. You can't be a levitator so you become an adulterer. You make tangible the distance, the separation, between us and you. In a way, on the day you prove to us, once and for all, that you cannot levitate, that's when you finally drift away.

• • •

You don't become petty criminals and hardcore drug users the moment Mom throws Van out for the last time. Your felonious slide is slow. By some miracle, the miracle of lavish motherlove, your crimes are largely victimless, and you're jailed for nonviolent offences—trespassing; retail theft; possession, of marijuana, of paraphernalia, of controlled substance. Your drugs are recreational, in the beginning, with gateways leading to ever-elevated gateways. First Dane, then you—and by you, I mean me—then Shawn. The drop back into poverty, however, is quick as shit. The 1980s come to an end, and we're on food stamps again. Now Van's gone, Mom says, there's gonna be changes. Yeah, Gail says, No rules. Shut up, Gail, Mom says. For one, we're gonna need to rent out the

Nintendo room. That's not a rule, Gail says, that's just how it's gotta be. And two, Mom says, you're gonna have to get a job, to help with bills. Also not a rule, Gail says. That's just life. Once again, Mom says, you're gonna have to be the man of the house. Think you're up to it? Can I count on you? She waits. She wants an honest answer.

On 18 October 2012, Mom's in town for Halloween, visiting my wife, Thisbe, and me, but mostly she's here to see her first grandson, two-year-old Sonne. The four of us, Sharon and Sonne, Thisbe and me, will begin what becomes an annual tradition. We dress up, according to Sonne's whim, for Zoo Boo at Binder Park in Battle Creek, Michigan, a small dying zoo in a dying Midwestern city, a city dependent upon a breakfast, cereal, fewer and fewer people eat.

We've got our costumes all set for Zoo Boo. Sonne determined we'd all be *Wizard of Oz*. The adults worked out the particulars. Mom will be the Lion. Thisbe will go as Dorothy, complete with ruby slippers she's fashioned from a pair of pumps doused with red glitter-paint. Sonne, as the Tin Man, will fit into a silver painted cat-litter box, a funnel tied atop his little head. I'm the Scarecrow, the cuffs of my sleeves and pants stuffed with straw pulled from the chicken coop. But Halloween's days away yet.

On the eighteenth, we're running an errand, returing a rental car, and I conduct an impromptu interievw of Mom. What follows is a verbatim transcript. While I stop transcribing at the six-minute mark, I redact nothing, maintaining all of our "ums" and "ahs," wanting to present—maybe you guessed it—the best copy available. However fucked up and unflattering. It does beg the question, though: What counts as *best*?

In our case, I think, *best* is what's most true. But *best* is not the Truth, capital T. Our divergent understandings of the Truth—our offspring little truths—get as near to what actually happened as possible. Our individual truths approach the

Truth. But the truth, as we each experience it, is only ever an approximation of the greater collective Truth. The universal Truth. What some might even go so far as to call reality.

The more we try to measure that gap between what happened and what we experienced, the more that gap opens. That's why the truth's so damn hard to defend. The truth gets confused by the delay between cause and effect. What actually happens can change with our perspective, can widen or reduce that gap, depending on where we're standing, in time or in space, because the farther away we get from events, the harder it becomes to determine both our own relative truths and the greater classical Truth.

No one knows this better than someone like Anthony Broadwater, the Black man who served sixteen years in prison for the rape of Alice Sebold, a white woman who wrote the memoir *Lucky* detailing her experience of her rape and its aftermath. The rape conviction proved, in the end, to be dead wrong, even if the rape itself was irrefutable. Sebold had her truth. Broadwater had his. Sebold showed, in the short term, that her truth proved more convincing. She relayed that truth with more passion and, it turns out, with some prejudice.

The entire justice system in Syracuse, New York, worked, sometimes nefariously, to corroborate Sebold's truth. Turns out, a young white woman is harder to disbelieve than a young Black man. No surprise there. But it was Broadwater's truth, less convincing in the tumult of the moment, that won out in the end, because Broadwater refused to give up on his version of events, and this truth of his proved to be nearer the Truth, capital motherfucking T. Anthony Broadwater's story is now the best copy we have available for his innocence, but his exoneration—tragic for everyone involved, but by no means equally tragic—has not brought Alice Sebold any nearer to discovering the true identity of her rapist or to bringing her sexual offender to justice.

• • •

In what follows, my mom recounts, in her own words, her rape. I hesitiate to call what follows *her truth*, because I've watched her truth change over time. This means it is not truth at all, not really. It is her opinion, her take, her assessement, her story. In the same way that I've got my story of what Richie did to me, which also isn't necessarily the truth. It is testimony, and not under oath. We, in our exceedingly self-important age, have come to conflate our story with the truth. Our story is *not* the truth, can never *be* the truth; our story can only ever be our telling of our experience of the truth. That is three degrees of remove. Sometimes, if we're lucky, if we're good and thorough and observant, patient and empathetic, our story can be true. But our story, despite the oaths we take and the promises we make, can never be the truth, the whole truth, and nothing but the truth. A story, any story, even a true story, can only ever be a copy.

• • •

Pay attention to the way my Q&A with Mom goes back and forth, and how, almost effortlessly, Mom turns the tables on me at the end. The investigator becomes the investigated.

My questions of her abuse lead us straight, and not surprisingly, into her questions of mine. All this while a two-year-old Sonne listens in, eating a grilled cheese sandwich.

Though I could, at first, only bring myself to transcribe the first six minutes—the conversation doesn't end, not as long as Mom and I are both alive—even if the conversation does have a beginning. It shares its beginning with this story you have here before you, 24 February 1984, a story that I've tried to fashion, maybe too desperately, into a three-way conversation, between the past, the present, and the future.

If our respective declines, of mother and son, follow the natural order, I imagine that on her deathbed, as I hold her hand, and I'm a sopping mess—I have her easy tears, though I don't laugh as readily—with her last breaths, she and I will be having some version of this very conversation, even if the only words either of us can manage are I love you. Maybe that abridgment—those three words—is the closest that either of us, that any of us, can ever come to the Truth.

• • •

A.   "That was like . . . that wasn't the bad part of it," Mom says. "It was the . . . punching."

Q.   Distractedly, I drive the rental car—I can't evoke what make and model—and Mom's in the back seat minding Sonne. With her consent, I've turned on a voice recorder. It's 2:39 p.m. EST. "And all this happened in the back seat?"

A.   ". . . punching in the face—no. It actually happened up on the ground outside the car." Mom and I share a long thirty-three-second silence. Sonne doesn't make a sound.

A.   Mom breaks the silence. "Yeah, then I got crabs!" She laughs and I join her, reluctantly, but her laugh has always been infectious, even when inappropriate. "So it was like—go find somebody that's got crabs. That's the guy. But I didn't know that for a couple of weeks. You know, so."

Q.   When she doesn't offer anything more, I say, "The problem is on an army base probably nine out of ten guys have crabs."

A.   "Yeah, yeah, I guess."

Q.   "And at some point," I say, "he started saying that he was going to stab you or kill you, with a knife?"

A.   "Yeah. He had said that right at the beginning, so."

Q.   "But you fought anyway?"

A.   "Yeah, well, when he was trying to get me out of the car—"

Q.   "Yeah."

A. "—into the back seat I figured that was my best chance." A moment later, she says to Sonne, "Let me see, you want more bread?"

A. Sonne, in an insanely adorable twenty-eight-month-old voice: "Choo cool busses."

Q. Mom says, "Two school busses?"

A. "Der were," Sonne says, "der were two *cool* busses." His high voice goes even higher with "cool." He's trying his hardest, I can imagine, to get his mouth to make that impossible S sound. In lieu of a hissing sibilant he's resorted to falsetto, the closest he can get.

Q./A. Mom says, "Two cool busses." And then ten seconds later: "You know and like, I don't know, I didn't even get hysterical. My whole thing was, you know, just get home and be with you guys. It's like," she laughs, "I don't have, I don't have the time to be hysterical." Laughing harder now. "Or not get my act together, you know."

Q. "Yeah," I say. "I guess that's the thing that's most . . . impressive and courageous to me is that like, you know, I've—" The car blinker comes on. "Ah, you know I very clearly remember being woken up by Gail and going to the army base and seeing, you know, how bruised and, and swollen your face was—"

A. "Hm, face was a mess."

Q. "—um, and then after that I don't, you know, I don't really have . . ." The blinker goes silent. ". . . much memory at all of um . . ."

A. "Trauma."

Q. "Yeah of any kind of trauma or any kind of lasting effect other than you know I think I was acutely aware of your, your fear of Black men—"

A. "Yeah."

Q. "—after that. And, and you know I thought, I thought it manifested, I thought it was a kind of racism, you know—"

A. "Oh sure."

Q. "—when I was a kid. I think, when, when I became . . . aware enough, ah, you know you were just telling us, or not just telling us, but you, you had told us that it was a, it was a mugging, just so we could probably deal with it and understand it and—"

A. "Yeah."

Q. "—and not, you know, start expressing it and exhibiting our own racism. You know, and fear of Black men."

A. "Yeah well I didn't want you to be afraid of 'em."

Q. "And I, I think that really worked, you know. Because I wasn't."

A. "Right."

Q. "Ah."

A. "You know and I tried to not be, you know, that way, even in New Jersey, after it happened, I was friends with Clarence, you know, would dance with him, and let him hug me and stuff, and Joe Randle—"

Q. "Clarence, Clarence Clemons?"

A. "Yea."

Q. "I remember Joe Randle."

A. "Yeah and Joe was another, you know, whether it was subconsciously or what, you know I sort of just, I don't know, trying to prove to myself you know I wasn't gonna be a racist." She laughs. "You know. But. And like and I wouldn't go, I don't know, you probably don't remember, but like in the winter time it was really hard cause I wouldn't even go like put the garbage out if I forgot to put the garbage out before dark, it didn't get put out. You know I wouldn't even walk down the edge of our driveway at night, so."

Q. "Yeah and I don't really remember that either."

A. "Yeah."

Q. "The only thing I really remember is, is the seeming racism, and I can remember instigating it a couple times, and I can remember when it came out—"

A. "Asking me, 'If I married a, what would you do —'"

Q. "Yeah."

A. "'—if I brought home a Black girl?' I wouldn't do, I wouldn't do nothing." She laughs.

Q. "Yeah and then I said, 'What would you do if, ah, I had a baby with a Black girl?'"

A. "Yeah."

Q. "And I can remember, we were coming home from the Outback and, so this was in Florida at that time so—"

A. "Umhm."

Q. "—probably like the late '80s, the early '90s, and I can just remember you crying."

A. She laughs.

Q. "Like you didn't respond to, to the further instigation, you just started crying. And then Gail was the one who said, 'You know your mom wasn't mugged that night, she was raped,' and then, you know, and I think I, I finally, didn't understand but all of it started to make sense to me."

A. "Umhm."

Q. "And I didn't, you know, I probably didn't understand until I was able to talk to you about, you know, about Richie and, and I, I think that time in, in Boston where we were able to have like an exchange as adults, you know, talking about our own experiences where—"

A. "Yeah."

Q. "—I think I gained some understanding."

A. "I wha—I couldn't understand about you and Richie why's you never told me about you and Richie, about Richie, in the beginning. You know I would've never, ever let him come near you again—" She laughs. "—if I would've known what was going on."

• • •

End of January, 2015, six months before I lose my mind, I get what I think is a phishing e-mail. I've been approached before by people on the hunt for my mom or one of my brothers, for our father. Often debt collectors. When a family member cuts losses—declares bankruptcy, defaults on a car or student loan, fails to pay income taxes, child support, or alimony for a decade or three—everyone in said family gets shaken down, with varying degrees of emotional and legal force, to see what jangles on out. These services are vaguely menacing, unnerving. Unfortunately, they remind me of home.

But this e-mail out of the blue, with its problematic grammar, seems less like a prank or debt collection, more like a scam—identity theft—and I'm tempted to fall for it, because why the hell not. It's winter in Michigan.

• • •

Jordan, John A CIV USARMY USACRC (US)   📁 Writing-Related   January 28, 2015 at 2:52 PM
FOIA request response (FA14-4230) (UNCLASSIFIED)
To: Jay Baron Nicorvo

Classification: UNCLASSIFIED
Caveats: NONE

Ms. Nicorvo, the information is going to be sent thru Safe Access File Exchange (SAFE) and may appear in your junk email. Please be advise that the from line on the email will be No-Reply@amrdec.army.mil. You will receive a password to access our response to your request.

John A. Jordan
Information Release Specialist
USACIDC Crime Records Center (FOIA)
Quantico Va 22554
phone: 571-305-4225

Classification: UNCLASSIFIED
Caveats: NONE

• • •

That the classification is UNCLASSIFIED and the caveats are NONE both strike me as nice touches. Here's the work of a practiced con artist. But I pause at the DOT spelling of thru, and the sentence that worries me—*Please be advise that the form line . . .* —sounds like the syntax of nineteen-year-old Dnipropetrovsk hacker writing in what is his fourth or fifth language. And that name, John A. Jordan, is too all-American to be believable. I mean, come on, John. What kind of a stooge do you take me for.

In my junk folder, delivered three minutes after John Jordan's e-mail, I find the follow-up, the first words of which are *Direct replies will not be read by a human.*

• • •

In the follow-up e-mail addressed to Mom but sent to me, "AMRDEC Safe Access File Exchange Delivery Notice," I read and reread the sentence: *If the reader of this message is not the intended recipient, you are hereby notified that any reading, dissemination, distribution, copying, or other use of this message or its attachments is strictly prohibited.*

I hover. My cursor poised over the supposed link to the file. I click on it. The browser opens, and a warning advises:

> This Connection Is Not Private—This website may be impersonating "safe.amrdec.army.mil" to steal your personal or financial information. You should close this page.

Understanding, vaguely, the risks involved—because, if you want to steal my identity, you can have it, and let's face it, I've never placed much value in my broke-ass financial information—I visit the website. Operated and hosted by the U.S. Army Aviation and Missile Research Development and Engineering Center (AMRDEC).

AMRDEC is—if the description at the bottom of the web-page is to be believed—*the Army's focal point for providing research, development, and engineering technology and services for aviation and missile platforms across the lifecycle.* I have little idea what any of this might be about—I grew up to be neither a rocket scientist nor an aeronautical engineer—but I'm fascinated. A little frightened. Somehow, my mom—and me by proxy—has been dragged into the U.S. government's web of domestic espionage.

Saying a prayer for my financial security, such that it is, and bidding my identity a nice-knowing-you, I hit "submit."

A PDF file titled "FA14-4230(E-MAIL RELEASE)" bounds into my downloads. Thinking I'm fucked, I try—and fail—to cancel the download. When the download's done, I stare at it. I drag-and-drop the file into my trash folder, but I don't empty the trash. I go back about my business. Problem is, I don't really have any business.

• • •

In Michigan in 2015, we're snowed in, and for the first time since age fourteen, I'm jobless. To come from a working-class family and to be without employment is nullifying. Unmanning. I feel like a gender defector and a class traitor. And the white-collar work I'd been doing for years wasn't even considered real work by my family. At the end of the fall, right before the holidays, I quit teaching at the university in Kalamazoo. The instructor's pay sucked and my wife, Thisbe, is tenured there—we get by on her salary—and we decided my time was better spent at home.

I do have work, I just don't have a job. I'm an ever-present father for Sonne, who's now five years old all the sudden, same age I was when I said goodbye to my father. In my down moments, I remind myself that I haven't become my absent father—at least not yet—and, in fact, I have become his exact opposite: son of a deadbeat dad become a stay-at-home dad.

In the mornings, often before everyone's awake, I write. But I don't have deadlines. I have chores. I do dishes. I cook and tidy. I take on our complicated taxes. Inspired by the Hanging Gardens of Babylon, I cultivate houseplants—half a dozen orchids, ivy, a flowering bougainvillea, a species of spiderwort formerly known as wandering Jew, grown partly for our son, a Jew according to rabbinical law—plants I pot and dangle from the rafters of the vaulted ceiling in our living room. I mow, take out the garbage. I keep our old farmhouse from falling on our sleeping heads or going up in flames, which can be a full-time job.

We're just north of Battle Creek, in among the cornfields, on a stretch of Baseline Road that, in fits and starts, runs like a broken thread clear across the Mitten State. With no irony, we call home Godsmark. The homestead was established in 1839, the modest farmhouse built in 1850, and the patriarch was a prominent Seventh-day Adventist, Richard Godsmark. The plat is a long stretch of wooded acres, reaching back to Waubascon Lake, that was ranch and orchard in Godsmark's time.

The Midwest is another frigid doozy after the historically snowy winter of 2014. We're breaking record lows for the second year running, this while Anchorage is getting balmy summertime temps, and our stockpile of firewood is dwindling. We keep our little Jøtul stove blazing twenty-four hours a day; our boiler, old as I am, burns propane, and even if we could afford to nudge the thermostats above sixty-five, the furnace couldn't do the work of heating the high-ceilinged house on its own.

Since Sonne started kindergarten, I have some more time. I build a chandelier out of a hay trolley. I read. I pile and split firewood I buy from sketchy pricks on craigslist, shysters trying to sell me doug fir as a hardwood. I shovel snow. From piled boulders an earlier owner of our house called the Divorce Circle, I stack cairns till my fingers go numb. I check to see that our dozen geriatric chickens haven't become poultry popsicles. And for days upon days, I keep coming back to that file in my trash folder.

One morning—I don't recall if I was feeling especially hopeful or hopeless—I open the thing.

No scam, it's the Goddamn answer to a Freedom of Information Act request I made a year and a half earlier on my mom's behalf. I'd forgotten all about the request, it took so long. I skim the cover letter:

> The names of law enforcement personnel . . . and other personal items of information pertaining to third parties have been withheld . . . a partial denial pursuant to Title 5, USC, Section 552, Exemptions (b)(6), and (b)(7)(C) of the FOIA.

Before closing the file—only to spend the next couple of months trying, and failing, to ignore its contents—I scroll quickly through.

• • •

I can't believe it. Here's the criminal investigation report generated out of that night. Ground wet, dark. What strikes me are all the redactions. Also, how most pages are stamped BEST COPY AVAILABLE and, in the title field, the reporting agent has typed Unknown; Rape and Sodomy. Then there's the bad black-and-white photocopy of a photo.

My mom's battered, barely recognizable face, half in darkness, makes me sob like a toddler.

• • •

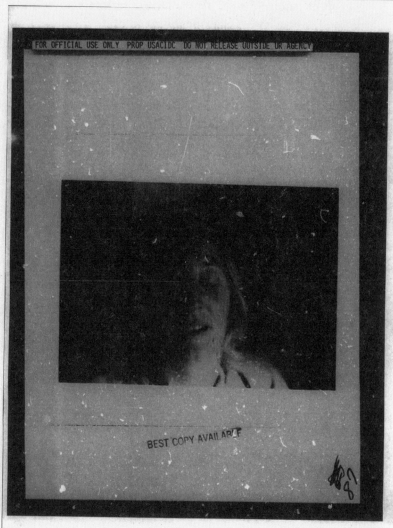

000086

I've spent most of my life piecing together the story of that night, 24 February 1984—while avoiding acknowledgement of my molestation—and when the official narrative of Mom's rape is delivered to my inbox, I can't bring myself to look at it.

Now, I'm faced with the fact that this night has a date, two days before Dane's fifth birthday. It has weather. It has pictures for fucksake.

I reopen the file, and scroll through, see that picture of my mom, half her face in shadow, and I sob, again. Again, I shut it down. Building up the courage? I don't think so. I might never reopen it. Because the file isn't mine to begin with, and according to the letter of the law, I'm committing a federal crime by simply having the file on my computer.

• • •

Did they ever catch the guy?

Isn't that what you're wondering? That, invariably, is the question I get when I mention my mom's rape, and it's one reason, in my middle age, I stopped mentioning it. The question reminds me how distorted, how nonsensical and nonlinear, my thinking about that night has turned.

In my twenties and thirties, I talked about Mom's rape with people I trusted. Girlfriends mostly, and I didn't have many. Seven by the time I met Thisbe. I've been, all my life, a strict monogamist. But after all this—from that night of the rape to the delivery of its recorded history into my inbox, spanning thirty years and 339 days, give or take—the question of justice has not just gotten lost. It's become irrelevant.

Mom feels the same way. Catching a criminal, solving a crime. That's some TV-show bullshit. The hokey hogwash of *Law & Order* reruns, or the compulsions of true crime podcasts.

Real life asks more pressing questions, panic-inducing, that the passage of time somehow seems to make more intense, not less.

Maybe it's because we can't stop remembering a night like that night. Each time we do, we warp it a little. What we're left with are our questions in the present, related to the past but distantly so, like, How in the fuck do I take out the trash after dark? Screw it, let it rot.

But *did* they ever catch the guy?

No, asshole, no they did not catch the fucking guy, ever.

And that question, the one I stopped asking myself, pulls me back—forcibly, through three decades obsessing over the stand-out details, details I recall, and details I was only able to coax from the adults around me with great difficulty.

The question, though, is important. I mean, how many other women have these men fucked up? How many children founder in their wake?

For my own sanity, and for my mom's, I long ago needed to move beyond any question of justice. Justice is a luxury most poor folks—not to mention most women, people of color, and kids—can't afford in this country.

Then, the investigation report arrives, and that question— did they ever catch the guy—comes roaring back to life.

I don't tell Mom at first. And I tell my mom everything. I live over a thousand miles away, but I see her half a dozen times a year or more, and she's my best friend aside from my wife.

These days, since I did my part to provide Mom with her first grandchild, we Skype once a week. I'm a mama's boy, and glad of it. That's one way Thisbe says she knew to marry me, knew I'd make a good father. As a father, I try to be my mom. But I can't tell Mom about the investigation report, not yet.

As winter of 2015 turns spring, I get more agitated poring over the pages. What I'm not prepared for is how the record of that time and of that place brings back not only details of my mom's sexual assault—unknown; *rape and sodomy*—but also the events surrounding my own.

• • •

My molestation ran concurrently with Mom's rape—for how long I can't be sure. I have three vivid memories of three separate occasions. Good things don't always come in threes, even if three is the magic number. Each of these triumvirate violations was more severe than the one that came before. They follow—maybe a bit too closely for comfort—what we writers call the rising action described by German novelist Gustav Freytag: introduction, rise, climax. Freytag plotted this dramatic movement in a pyramid. After the climax comes the return or fall, followed by catastrophe. And that's the end. Freytag didn't do dénouement.

I can't know if there were other occasions of abuse. I can't be sure there weren't fewer. But I'd bet my life on my recall of those three nights.

And, no, motherfucker, they didn't catch Richie either, who was a minor at the time. Given his age, he can never be charged, no matter that New Jersey amended their statute of limitations for sex abuse. All this is circumstantial anyway. There is no proof. Merely an absence of verifiable fact. Remember, this is not the truth. It is only a story.

As a way to overwhelm the inchoate, undocumented nature of my abuse, I throw myself into my mom's. Maybe my hope is that if I can come to know Mom's case, it'll help me to know my own. I even catch myself thinking—insanely—maybe I can catch my mom's rapist.

• • •

NICORVO *related that she worked for Dominoes Pizza and had delivered a pizza to bldg 1200E. About 1220AM she had exited and returned to her car which had been parked outside, unlocked. She got in, sat down and started the car up. Someone's right arm then came over her shoulder and around her neck, pulling her back against the seat. The man said, "If you don't do what I tell you, I'm going to kill you." He then told her* to drive ahead. NICORVO replied I can't you're choking me. He then directed her to the big parking lot at the end of the street, telling her, "If you do anything wrong I'll kill you". He then told her to stop the car between two trailers and tried to pull her over the front seat into the back seat. NICORVO said she couldn't fit over the the seat and struggled to get out of the car. He said, "You're going to get it now". He was still holding her with his right hand. She bit his right hand and tried to slam the door on his arm. She then got away and started to run. He caught her and dragged her back to the parking lot. She was flat on her back with the guy kneeling over her, trying to get her pants off. He had a hard time, not realizing that the pants were elastic waist, but he finally got them off one leg. He then told her to suck his penis and that she better get it hard or "I'll kill you". "You have a minute to make it hard." He forced his penis into her mouth and while she was gagging, he said, "Do you like it". The guy had one hand over NICORVO's eyes pressing her head against the ground. He then got on her and told her to put it in. He tried to put it in but couldn't get an erection. He tried a couple of pumps, got up, and then ran. NICORVO related that he didn't ejaculate and that she only knew that he was black by his penis being black. He had told her that he had a knife but she did not see one. After he ran she got up from the parking lot, ran to her car, got in, locked the doors, put her pants on and drove to the West Gate. NICORVO described the suspect as: black male, 6' tall, average build, light short jacket (possibly tan), light colored pants, caribbean accent, short hair, middle twenties. NICORVO could not recall seeing his face and therefore would not recognize him if she saw him. NICORVO further related that during the struggle in the car that she had bitten his right thumb, unsure if she broke the skin, and that she had closed the door on his right arm. At times during the interview NICORVO was laughing, crying and subdued as typical of someone recovering from shock.

• • •

In the ROI (Report of Investigation) there exist three distinct AIRs (Agent's Investigation Reports). There's the first, AIR I, of 29 February 1984, in which he details the initial notification of this offense and actions taken during crime scene processing and the preliminary investigation. The second, AIR II, of 26 March 1984, *details the interviews of suspects and witnesses, and other investigative activity in connection with this investigation.* The final, AIR III, of 12 July 1984, documents *coordination with MPs and civilian police, other interviews and the closure of the investigation.* Given the redactions, I can't know for certain that the three reports were all written by the same agent. But after a comparison of the handwriting of the agent who signed and dated each AIR, I suspect there is only one author. His 2s, 8s, and 4s give him away.

• • •

There are versions of that night. They're not competing. They come together—and continue to do so, even after all this is said and done—making a triptych picture that can never be complete. The versions I'm acquainted with are relayed—or *related*, to use the investigating agent's word—by three people.

We have the anonymous special agent conducting the investigation, his name redacted. We get some sense of him, his sober attempts at objectivity, wanting not to sully the facts with himself. There's a prudishness to him—*he tried to put it in*—even a hint of grim satisfaction—*but couldn't get an erection*—an element of, what, skepticism? racism?—*she only knew that he was black by his penis being black*—and a final, pitiful stab at sympathy—NICORVO *was laughing, crying and subdued as typical of someone recovering from shock*—well no shit, you insensitive cunt.

Then there's my version. This is tricky, and I have a reputation for being something of a trickster. But on the page, I do my damnedest to be earnest, and truthful to a fault. I'm cagey, withholding, but openly so. In my adulthood, I loathe sarcasm, can't stomach irony. I do not lie. Snark sickens me. I am at home in the heartfelt Midwest. And yet, here, on the page, I find myself at the far other end of our sincere special agent.

Let's call him Special Agent Redacted. Where Agent Redacted does his best to be objective, I'm doing my best to expose, and even amplify, my subjectivity, lest it be overlooked. I'm like Hunter S. Thompson covering the reelection campaign of that cocksucker Nixon. (Since age eighteen, I've borne a tattoo inspired by the flag-adorned skull on the original cover of Thompson's *Fear and Loathing: On the Campaign Trail '72*. I did ask the artist to omit the swastikas from the eyes of the skull.) Unlike Thompson, I'm trying to be a good father and husband first. I am gonzo lite. I do no drugs, these days. I'm not only implicitly biased, I am motherfucking compromised—this is my mom we're talking about, assholes—and I need my bias to be explicit.

The editorializing is, obviously, mine. The swearing, that's me, even if in my day-to-day life I rarely resort to profanity. I choose and order the information, with approval and input from my mom. (She could do without all the dirty fucking words.) And I do, in the end, have my own living memory of that night—seen, heard, and felt through the dark, echoey tunnel of three decades and counting. Lastly, I have a terribly intimate relationship with the aftermath.

If Agent Redacted and I stand in oppostion, my mom is not in the middle. Mom and her rape exist apart from any telling.

After Agent Redacted conducted his interview—about ninety minutes following the rape—but before he wrote and dated his report of the interview—five months and two days following the rape—he asked her to give a sworn statement.

That statement, taken down by an official the day following the rape, is as close as we can get to the rape, but it's still nowhere near rape. Not even close. It's a story. A story can do little more than hint at life. A story—even a great one—is but a shadow of the events that cast it. Flat. Monochrome.

Notice the discrepancies between my mom's sworn statement the day after her rape and the agent's report of the interview the night of.

Mom's version of events, too, is tricky, because she and I have been talking about this night, off and on, since that night. I've heard countless retellings. They change over time, as far as I recall, and my recall for who says what to whom is not normal. It's uncanny.

• • •

I, Sharon Nicorvo, want to make the following statement under oath: About 1220 a.m., 24 Feb 84, I delivered a Pizza to Bldg 1200 east, Ft Monmouth, NJ, to a guy named [redacted] I think. He came down to the [ ] desk and paid by check. I then left the building and returned to my car. I got in the car and shut the door. Then this big arm came around my throat and a guy said "If you don't do as I say I'll kill you, I have a knife". He then made me drive out of the parking lot. We turned left and started towards the main parking lot. He kept threatening to kill me. As we entered the parking lot, he still had his right arm around my throat choking me and with his left hand he steered the car to the right between two trailers. He made me stop the car and park there. Then he told me to get in the back seat. I said that I can't. He then tried to pull me over the seat into the back. That is xxx when he started to lose his grip on my neck. I had my left hand on the door so I just went to get out of the car. I slip under his arm and he then just had a hold of my right arm. He was then trying to hold me and get out of the back door. I was trying to still get out of the front door and also hold the back door shut. He the[ ]it my right hand and I leaned back into the car and swung the soda rack at xxxx[ ]xx his face with my left hand. Then I got further out of the car with only my right arm inside and me still holding the back door shut. I then bit his right thumb, the hand holding my hand, and he let go. I then ran screaming towards the gate house out of the parking lot. He caught up with me and started to beat me by hitting me in the face xxxx and head with his hand or fist. Then he pulled me back into the parking lot. I'm not sure how he had a hold on me. He then tripped me with his foot and knocked me to the ground. He then straddled me on xx his knees with his hand over my face telling me not to look at him. He had his xxxxxxxxxxxxxxxxx right hand over my face holding my head against the pavement and he was trying to take my pants off with his left hand. He kept telling me to xxx take them off and I told him that I can't and I won't.

xxx I could not move any part of my body, except my legs. He then got my elastic waist pants over and off my left leg. Then he told me to suck him and make him hard. He said if I bit him xhe would kill me or stab me. He then forced his penus into my x mouth. I was trying to do what I was told but I was gagging. He xxxxxxxxx said why can't you do this right, you can do better than this. I was choking and gagging. He then said that I had one minute to make it hard. He then took his penus out of my mouth and put his hand back over my face and xxx moved down. He was then telling me to put it in. He was laying on top of me and I still couldn't move. He was then putting it in and he said "I better come xx or your dead. You've got thirty seconds to make me come." He tried to put his penus into my vagina twice but it wouldn't stay in. I think that it wouldn't stay in because of the position that he was in on me and that it wasn't hard. He just tried two humps and then said you don't know how to fuck and got up. He ran away towards the field across the road. I got up and ran to the car. I got in and locked the doors. xxxxxxxxxxxxxxxxx I started the car and drove away from that area and stopped on the road in front of the 1200 building where there was a light. I opened the door so I could put my leg into my pants. I put them on and drove to the guard house.

Q.   Would you describe the guy?
A.   Black male, about 6', average build, in his twenties, caribbean accent, light colored short xx jacket and pants, short hair.
Q.   Would you be able to recognize him again?
A.   No.
Q.   Had you earlier in the evening delivered a pizza to anyone of this description or had any problems with anyone?
A.   No. I had been delivering earlier to the 200 area. I may have been to xx the 1200 west once that night but I can't remember.
Q.   Did you ever see a knife?
A.   No.
Q.   Did he say anything that you thought unusual?
A.   Yes right in the beginning while driving he said something like "I'm sick and tired of this, I can't take xxxxxxxxx this shit anymore." I didn't know what he was talking about.
Q.   Where was the soda rack that you swung at his x face?

A.   Right next to the pizza box setting on the front seat.

Q.   Did he say anything to you as he was chasing you?

A.   He was yelling "your asking for it now. Now your really going to get it. I'm just going to have to kill you now."

Q.   Did you break the skin when you bit his hand?

A.   I don't know.

Q.   Could you tell if the guy had been circumsized?
                 xxxxxxxxxxxxxxxx

A.   Maybe not, I don't think he was though. I never seen anyone not circumcised though.

Q.   Did he have a condom on?

A.   No.

Q.   xxx Did his accent seem natural or could he have been faking it?

A.   It seemed natural, I never thought at any time that he was trying to disguise it.

Q.   Could you detect anything like after shave or was he a smoker?

A.   xxxxxxxxxxxxxxxxxxxxxx There was no distinct smell that I recall. I don't smoke and I think I would have noticed that smell.

Q.   Would you like to add anything to this statement pertaining to this matter?

A.   No.///END OF STATEMENT///

• • •

What does it say about me—as a man, a son, a victim of sexual abuse, a hack private dick—that one question I come back to, over the next months and years even, in regard to my mom's statement under oath, is not about my mom or her assailant?

One nagging question I have is about the official who recorded my mom's statement: What sort of person thinks that the word we share in English for a man's sex organ is spelled penus?

I can't let this go, this misspelling. I try to claim it. Make it my own. I even come to read a directive into it, a commandment: pen us. That is, write us. That, or: contain us. Fence us in. And the more I write it, penus, the more normal it looks.

• • •

I read *My Dark Places* in a few murderous days, days obliter-
ated by my obsessive reading. I'm astounded. Dispirited.
What James Ellroy does in that book is dive face first into the
emptied-out pool of the murder of his mother, who was strangled with her stocking when Ellroy was all of ten. In middle
age, early forties, Ellroy gets his hands on his mother's murder file and turns that record into a course of action. There is
little talk. No time for commas. The rumination is distilled.
The book tears ass from one investigative doing to the next.
Me, what do I do? I turn a criminal report into a soliloquy. Ellroy goes like Othello seeking answers. I'm most interested in
asking questions. Never mind if they're right. Answers would
be nice, and Ellroy's insights are hidden like contraband in
among all the names, dates, and details of his inquiry. When
he does flash them, you see they're shivs he's fashioned out of
short sentences he stabs—occasionally, unexpectedly—into
the reader's eye.

By writing that book, Ellroy was teaching himself how to
love his mother and, in turn, value women. He's trying to
free himself from the shackles of misogyny, something that
his profession, the crime novelist, trades in, because the rape
and murder of women and girls—and how well those stories
sell—is an indictment of our misogynist culture. But I don't
have Ellroy's problem. Motherlove is maybe the one thing I've
never lacked, and I've been lucky in my love of, for, and by
women. My problem is manlove. My problem is my father.
My problem is me.

• • •

Of course every short-haired Black man standing near six feet
tall is immediately and automatically a suspect in Mom's rape,
soldiers and civilians alike, and on 28 February 1984, just before lunch, a doctor of social welfare at Patterson Army Com-

munity Hospital, rank of major, contacts Agent Redacted, stating that he *would do anything he could to assist this office and further related that he had some information that he felt should be discussed with a representative of this office.*

Fifteen minutes later, Agent Redacted interviews the major, *who advised that this office should consider as a suspect, Dr. (Gynocologist) [redacted] of Patterson Army Community Hospital. Dr. [redacted] is a black male with a pronounced Carribian accent. [Redacted] reported that during a lunchtime conversation amoung a group of doctors, conversation had turned to the subject of [redacted] not being "able to get it up" (experiencing erectile dysfunction) with his girl friend during a recent vacation. The conversation was good natured but [redacted] is concerned that the discussion indicated behavior consistant with the behavior of the perpetrator of this offense.*

Agent Redacted pursues this lead but, to his credit, only so far, not even bothering to trouble the suspected doctor with an interview. Instead, later that same afternoon, he coordinates with another special agent in the office of the U.S. Army Criminal Investigation Command: *Dr. [redacted] fully identified as LTC [redacted] USA MFDDAC, is the doctor that was called to examine NICORVO after the rape and is the man that she refused to allow to examine her because he was black. [redacted] further reported that [redacted] is only 5'9" tall.* The report makes no further mention of Dr. [redacted].

There's something reassuring in reading to discover that, for Special Agent Redacted at least, the determining characteristic of the doctor is neither his Caribbean accent nor the color of his skin. It's his height. And, too, that the agent in charge of the investigation is less bigoted than the accusing doctor, whose suspicions are aroused by the simple fact of a Black colleague with an accent and erectile dysfunction.

But can you imagine being my mom in that situation?

About 0338, 24 February 1984, she sits in an examination room at Patterson Army Community Hospital (PACH). She's just been pummeled and raped, her life repeatedly threatened. She wants nothing more than to get home to her three little boys. She waits on the arrival of the OB/GYN. She's been on base for nearly four hours. Her multiple contusions of the skull have been treated. Her lacerated thumb—where her rapist bit her—is bandaged.

Two hours before her physical exam, Mom is interviewed, at length, by the assigned special agent. From out of that interview comes a description: *suspect is a black male, caribbean accent, wearing a field jacket.*

In a moment Mom will subject herself to the examination that yields twenty-one exhibits. They are as follows:

1. *Gauze pad with blood.*
2. *Gauze pad with blood.*
3. *Gauze pad with blood.*
4. *Orange, white, blue jacket.*
5. *Orange, white shirt.*
6. *Vaginal speciman, two swabs and two slides.*
7. *Envelope containing fingernail scrapings, left.*
8. *Envelope containing fingernail scrapings, right.*
9. *Envelope containing cut pubic hair.*
10. *Envelope containing cut head hair.*
11. *Envelope containing cut fingernails. Right hand*
12. *Envelope containing cut fingernails, left.*
13. *Plastic bag with combed pubic hairs.*
14. *Saliva stain.*
15. *Pulled head hairs.*
16. *Pulled pubic hairs.*
17. *Tube of blood.*
18. *Blue pants.*
19. *Blue blouse.*
20. *Beige sweater.*
21. *Beige panties.*

And here, knocking and then opening the door of the examination room for her vaginal exam, comes a Black male military doctor who greets my mom with a Caribbean accent.

Mom refuses.

After another doctor is summoned and performs the examination, at about 0430, Agent Redacted takes Mom back to the crime scene, where an MP patrol is *currently protecting a footprint*. Before Mom is brought back to the hospital, where we'll meet her in the waiting area before sunrise, she's asked to re-enact the rape for the agent, who takes notes:

> A check of the footprint being protected by the MPs revealed it to be a partial impression in the grass. There was no print observable. Photos were exposed in an attempt to determine size. There was nothing else of evidentiary value found at the scene.

· · ·

I can't catch my mom's rapist. What am I thinking? If James Ellroy couldn't catch his mother's killer by the end of *My Dark Places*, I've got zero chance of collaring my mom's rapist. I am no Ellroy. My places seem dimly lit by comparison. I'm more a Maggie Nelson, in *The Red Parts*, with a penus and a twenty-year-old copy of Eldridge Cleaver's rapist memoir, *Soul on Ice*. My parts aren't even red. They're faded pink. I'm a poor man's poor imitation of Maggie Nelson. I'm in drag as Maggie. Even if I could nab Mom's rapist, maybe I wouldn't want to. For all of America's countless Emmett Tills falsely accused, what if we just let my mom's rapist walk? And what if this, here, is just one more "Open Casket" act of appropriation? White rape spectacle? Then there's Till's mom, Mamie Till, who coauthored the memoir *Death of Innocence: The Story of the Hate Crime That Changed America*, and who imparts:

> It is not that I dwell on the past. But the past shapes the way we are in the present and the way we will become what we are destined to become. It is only because I have finally understood the past, accepted it, embraced it, that I can fully live in the mo-

ment. And hardly a moment goes by when I don't think about
Emmett, and the lessons a son can teach a mother.

And also:

Strong women don't merely birth children. They cultivate them
to render service.

Might that be what this is, the self-flagellation of this writing? Is this my sorry excuse for a service rendered? The best
copy I can make available for all to see, much as it pains me,
much as it shames me, much as it is driving me out of my
fucking mind? Because when Mrs. Till was questioned about
the wisdom of an open-casket viewing for her lynched son
and the devastation done to his sweet, fourteen-year-old face,
she said, "Let the people see what I've seen."

• • •

If Mom's right in her description, that in 1984 her rapist was
in his middle twenties, he would be about sixty at the time of
this writing. Too many years have passed. Too much information has been withheld or obscured, destroyed or lost. Mom
has moved on. I don't have the resources—financial, emotional—to collar a rapist over thirty years after the rape. Fort
Monmouth doesn't even exist anymore. It's a ghost base. In
2005, the post was tapped by the Base Realignment and Closure Commission. Army functions and personnel were scattered to the four bureaucratic corners. A closure ceremony
was held on 15 September 2011.

But if I can't catch the guy, I can try to imagine him, and in
so doing, capture him.

Because the rapist's side of my mom's rape is critical. He,
too, has a truth. Maybe his version of events is even more crucial than my mom's, callous as that sounds. The rapist is the

active agent. He's the cause, and Mom's the effect. If another woman delivered that pizza, my mom wouldn't've been raped. Someone else's mother would've. Rapists gonna rape, right?

If that rapist didn't exist—or if he did exist but had been raised with a love for, an admiration of, a pride in his mother, his sister, his aunt—well, what then? In that case, then no one's mother gets raped that night. And maybe in order to reach such a point of pride in women, and for women, we men must work to see not just the worst in other men but the worst in ourselves. I take it as my obligation to imagine—to occupy, even—my mom's rapist.

Picture him today. Living in Asbury Park. He's got a small business near the beach. Nothing fancy. Let's say it's a tire shop. Online, you can see the place gets decent reviews. He's married. Why not, right? Rapists marry. I want to say his wife's from Philly, I don't know why. City of Brotherly Love, maybe. She could be white or Black, both or neither. He's got kids. Three daughters. This is not outrageous. Rapists make babies. Chances are, half the babies are girls. And it was the birth of his first daughter—even more than his marriage to his wife, who sometimes asks him to play a little rough—that broke him of his most destructive desires. But his anger, his fear, these do rear up on occasion.

We can even go and read the reviews of his tire business. They're mostly positive (3.8 average stars) but then every third or fourth customer will have a negative experience:

> I politely explained to the employee exactly what I mentioned in the previous paragraph and asked to talk to a manager (which turned out to be the owner). Again, I politely explained the situation and was told "well, I can take $5 off." I told him fine, I'll pay it because what choice do I have, but that would mean that I wouldn't be coming back. At that point, he LOST HIS MIND. He said "just take the F'ing (he used the full word) car and get out." I told him that I'd be happy to pay a fair price but was told

"get the F out." I was stunned, and I said "wow, you're nuts," to which he replied "go F yourself." I have never been treated so unprofessionally, and I will be strongly suggesting to anyone interested in my opinion to buy their tires elsewhere.

These bouts of balled frustration are reserved for the occasional customer—always a fuckass white man, now that he thinks about it—but more than frustration, it's his feeling he's owed. Forty acres and a Ford, at least. Fuck. Too much has been kept from him in this country because of the simple, stupid color of his skin. Refuse to give reparations? We will take raperations. 'Cause it's like the brother Eldridge Cleaver, former Minister of Information for the Black Panthers, preaches in Soul on Ice: Rape was an insurrectionary act. It delighted me that I was defying and trampling upon the white man's law, upon his system of values, and that I was defiling his women—and this point, I believe, was the most satisfying to me because I was very resentful over the historical fact of how the white man has used the black woman. And: One thing that the judges, policemen, and administrators of prisons seem never to have understood, and for which they certainly do not make any allowances, is that Negro convicts, basically, rather than see themselves as criminals and perpetrators of misdeeds, look upon themselves as prisoners of war, the victims of a vicious, dog-eat-dog social system that is so heinous as to cancel out their own malefactions: in the jungle there is no right and wrong. If Mom's rapist did, once upon a time, choose to take what wasn't his, and by force, well, he could be forgiven. Couldn't he? That's what he tells himself, anyway—or, rather, that's what I imagine he tells himself. That's what I'd tell myself if I were him.

• • •

These men—my mom's rapist, my molester, my murderer un-uncle—they become one man. My greatest fear—the fear that not only keeps me up at night but that pushes me over the edge in my middle age—is that the one man they become is me.

• • •

Here're scraps of John Berger I cling to: *The past is never there waiting to be discovered, to be recognized for exactly what it is. History always constitutes the relation between a present and its past. Consequently, fear of the present leads to mystification of the past. The past is not for living in; it is a well of conclusions from which we draw in order to act.* And: *What I did not know when I was very young was that nothing can take the past away: the past grows gradually around one, like a placenta for dying.*

• • •

Mom's rapist, right before he raped her, said, "I'm sick and tired of this, I can't take xxxxxxxxxx this shit anymore." My murderer un-uncle, right before he chopped open Poppop's forehead with a butcher knife, said, "I've had it. I can't take any more." I don't re-member Richie ever saying he couldn't take any more. Have I ever said I can't take any more? Did I just say it?

• • •

> A.   "I wha—I couldn't understand about you and Richie why's you never told me about you and Richie, about Richie, in the beginning. You know I would've never, ever let him come near you again—" She laughs. "—if I would've known what was going on."
> A./Q.   "Cause he, you know, made us promise not to."
> Q.   "Yeah."
> A.   "You know, and, and Richie, you know, he was abusive. He used to punch us a lot, hard. Ah, over, you know, I mean I can remember, we would, a few times, we would walk from our house to Gail's, or from Gail's to our house—"
> Q.   "No."
> A.   "Yeah, yeah, a few times we did. A couple times we did. Um."

Q. "Oh, yeah, I guess after yous got a little older—"

A. "Yeah. Yeah, and it wasn't—"

Q. "—you would go to Richie's 'cause you could go to the beach and stuff like that."

A. "Yeah, I mean it wasn't that far. What was it, a mile or two?"

Q. "Couple miles. Yeah, a mile or two."

A. "Along Ocean Boulevard?"

Q. "Yeah."

A. "Yeah, 'cause—and we would walk—"

Q. "Cause I know yous would go that way with Rachel sometimes."

A. "And we would walk back, and he would ah, he would quiz us on all the makes and models of cars going by—"

Q. Mom laughs.

A. "—and if we got it wrong, he would, he would punch us. Um, you know, and—"

Q. "You and Dane?"

A. "Yeah. And I think mostly me." Sonne makes a sound: "Kah."

Q. "Okay," Mom says to him. "You done?"

A. "Deah."

A. "You know, and," I continue, "I, I should've told you but, I didn't not tell you because you know I was actively withholding something from you. I was, you know, he, he scared me—"

Q. "Right, right."

A. "—and so, I did what he said."

Q. "Yeah. And that's what they do. Unfortunately."

● ● ●

I spend days doing nothing. Listening to the portion of the audio file I've yet to finish. Setting out, sitting down, to transcribe the couple of minutes that remain. Then I spend the next few hours rereading the report of investigation. Or staring out the window. It looks onto our garden meadow. I watch one of our cats take a shit under the lilac bushes. I decide I just can't put myself through any more transcription about my molestation. It's too hurtful. Too numbing. It'll ruin my month. It'll cost me years. I'll pay a service. I'll use some app.

Online, I discover 360converter.com and upload my audio file. A minute later a program spits out a transcript. It is, for some unfathomable algorithmic reason, formatted like a poem. The transcript gives me some confidence that neither prose writers nor poets will be immediately supplanted by artificial intelligence, at least not in 2015. I alter next to nothing of what follows. If the machine were pressed to give it a title, I can imagine the non-sentience coming up with something like "Song of Unbelievable Lasers."

• • •

~~~~~~~ they think many children are
there are no longer afraid that you're going to be
that
I'm not afraid
and you were [SMACK] sharon
could you would do that
yet still have that concern that here you know any
time
and fledged anger
but just give you a automatic anger
[SMACK] like in those best
i don't act ~~~~~~ i think
the power of the room i don't think ~~~~~~ that
the them
was stealing
we did it now
but I'll make I'm going to be like that so easily mom
and i was like to do something ~~~~~~

and twice
and it was never there
was never essential
out of ways but this is golden opened and which
them [SMACK]
we were
just kids to you know
i imagine a version of myself
not make unconscious effort to avoid
those trapping
has not being a self for errors i i
you know and that going to [UM] abuse and child
and it makes sense
that is it's much harder to imagine now that i have a
child yeah
the next he was a fear would have been there before
you just because they see with people like to people
that are blown up
in the house with abuse of father being whether that
but they do when then get married you know i mean
it is a cycle
well the theme that i worry about now i mean it's
my fear now is
forever [SMACK] [UM] six like hear those statistics
[SMACK] about like now them for the last
generation
more than half of all very use to my home tomato in
summer
if you look closely of those statistics you see it
for the people who very in our thirties ~~~~~~~
have very and both have
do it degree use it can see someone a couple
like is in the in our demographic the chances
are like the percentages like got some divorce or
something like twenty percent ~~~~~~~ ~~~~~~~

if you're older and if you're better educated intend
to stay together ~~~~~~~
the
[UH]
~~~~~~~ [UM]

• • •

Which transcription is better, mine or the bot's? The bot gets
at something more true than I do, that's for sure. The bot-
generated words make me feel crazy; my words make me feel
sane. At the time, crazier is nearer the truth.

I give up my attempts to solve my mom's rape. The case is
cold. The U.S. Army Criminal Investigation Command can't,
or won't, track down the box of evidence, which may have
been destroyed with the closing of Fort Monmouth. The special agent in charge, Kimberly R. Bailey, stops returning my e-
mails or calls. I quit transcribing my interview with Mom. I'm
sick and tired of this. I can't take this shit any more. I've had
it. I can't take any more. It is finished.

• • •

On the day I lose my mind, 20 August 2015, the day before
Mom visits for my birthday, a boy rakes snaking paths through
our Godsmark woods, hour after hour. Wearing nothing but a
bathing suit, eight-year-old Mikey grabs my hand and pulls
me insistently from my task. I'm taking you with me, he says.
One of three children visiting for the day, along with his parents, he might well be talking to the rusty rake, borrowed
from us, that he drags in his other hand.

Having shucked his shoes, traipsing through acres of poi-
son ivy leaves painting him invisibly from toe to knee, he
won't let go of me. He bumps his hip into mine. He nuzzles
affectionately, if stiffly, into my side.

Skittering rake tines jangle my nerves. The manic-depressive weather is breezy and cool for a late-August after-noon, keeping back the bugs, but Mikey's been out here so long, the mosquitoes have zeroed in. They ride the moveable feast of him, raising warm welts on his brown skin. Stupidly I ask, You getting bitten?

He seems not to notice. All the ants, he says. Ants are under the leaves. I rake the leaves, not the ants. Ants you know have slaves.

Mikey is smart, observant, and wildly imaginative. His mind is deep and disordered. Nonverbal until age four, he was placed in foster care and, shown some true love, his stunted expressiveness bloomed. Half Black and at the severe end of the autism spectrum, he'd been adopted by two white West Coast lesbians, friends of Thisbe's, one a public-school librarian, the other a licensed clinical child psychologist who founded a renowned disability clinic for children and their families.

• • •

Mikey spent the first four years of his life locked in a cellar he was never allowed to leave, save for visits up to his grandfather, who regularly raped him.

After his years in a doting nontraditional family offering access to the best education and care, Mikey is developing in extraordinary ways, not all of them normal. Nagging voices, hallucinations, intractable obsessions.

I'm a middle-aged white man dragged through woods at the insistence a Black boy raised by two white lesbians, and I'm seeing so much of myself in Mikey that I start to lose the line dividing us. He's not crazy, he's just a kid, a tortured kid. A raped kid. But he comes across crazy, and in the company of crazy—or what seems crazy—I feel crazy.

Then comes my telltale fear. That's what sends me to the edge, my edge, and over. Inside the house, there are three smart, caring, and intensely independent women. And I'm suddenly certain that all three of them suspect I've taken Mikey into the woods to rape him.

I'm able to mumble, I love all the work you've done, Mikey. But I gotta get back to the house. To run errands. I yank my hand from his. I leave him wandering there—unfazed by mosquitoes, surrounded by ivy—trying to talk sense into his rake.

• • •

I'm shaking. In our normally docile kitchen gone chaotic with two other kids of wildly divergent backgrounds, plus the one I abandoned in the woods, parented by a pair of middle-aged women in a nonnuclear family using deep generosity, committed service, and all-inclusive love to passively yet decisively overwhelm the patriarchy; as my only boy-child cries possessively over shared Legos; but before the screen door slams, startlingly, behind me; as I'm peppered with questions—about the location of long-lost toys and the temperaments of our backyard hens—why no rooster; I beheaded him and we ate him—their breeds and names, ages, pedigrees, and politics—the three Rhode Island Reds, Trotsky, Lenin, and Stalin, are filthy communists—and the whereabouts of their surreptitious egg laying; as Laura, the psychologist, and Tara, the librarian, tell Thisbe, the novelist, stories about their Portland friends, lesbians all, and their broods of children begat by a Portland sperm bank, children who all look dismayingly alike, as if the bank has but one bottomless deposit to draw upon, jerked from a blond-haired, blue-eyed donor; how it's so lovely to see us and have an honest-to-God man around for the boys to interact with, a real man raised by two women, as I was, and nice especially for Glenn, the oldest at thirteen, who sits fidgeting in the kitchen, fussing like a newbie midwife over his expectant pimples, making mention of his third and fourth moms (from Laura's marriage before Tara), how he's a matriarchal man, like me, yes, like me, like me; and as I try to remember the breeds of the fifteen hens, Blue Splash Maran, Red Frizzle, Mille Fleur d'Uccle, and their ages, menopausal Beebee the oldest at nine; and whether or not the subtext of all this Henny Penny small talk is the insinuation that I sexually assaulted one of their sons in the woods; which of course I did not do, could not do, would never do, because I have lived in constant, crippling fear, and for ages, that those who learn I am a man who was molested as a child will come to assume—automatically, eventually—I'm bound to become a child molester; that this, right here, is the introductory scene of my intervention, if I would only acknowledge it; and oh shit the lit grill I left untended to be coaxed into those madding woods by a charmingly weird boy with, like me, like me, a history of childhood sexual abuse; and again with the names of the chickens, Oyster, Mapes, Ebony Spleenwort; and the children, whose names are further from me than the chickens', Mikey, Glenn, and Ayla, how I have forgotten Ayla, and of course our Sonne—yes, Sonne; no, Sonne; oh I don't know, Sonne—Sonne, crying, wearing his Captain America muscle suit, barefoot, wants to know where his harmonica is; and when I say who knows, he asks after the Lego piece with the thing and the thing that attaches to the thingy; and that's when Thisbe hands me a list of sundries that need fetching from the store for dinner: rolls, maybe those little balls of fresh mozzarella if they have them, our CSA veggies, some scrawled word that starts with S and looks like shasta or sherpa or shanti—om shanti shanti shanti—and it's here I lose it altogether. This is the moment I go mad.

• • •

I'm spiraling. I'm not losing the center. The vertiginous force I feel is not outward and away; it's centripetal. I'm not going to pieces—all the pieces are coming to me. To combat the repetitive and dizzying dread, I say, I feel panicked. I announce this to the kitchen.

The domestic chaos halts; it's as though I've thrown the merry-go-round emergency brake.

Brassy and beautifully butch, raised Catholic and forced to buck God and family both to blaze her own honest way, Tara's half out of our kitchen door. She's saying, in all earnestness, not her usual high-school-librarian register, Oh, Jay, do you want we should go?

I follow her onto the covered porch overlooking all the perennials Thisbe's cultivated: black-eyed Susan, blue false indigo, cosmos. Shaking my head in the shade, my mouth turning down on its own, I bulldoze Tara with the intimate news that, like Mikey, I was molested as a child. I tell Tara that, in the company of her kids—Ayla was also sexually abused by relatives—I'm experiencing flash after disorienting flash of my molestation.

But I'm incapable of confessing my worst concern: that she, her wife, and mine are all convinced that I'm bound by the vicious cycle of abuse—I must be a molested child molester.

I don't want you to go, I say. But I need you to know how your being here's bothering me. And by bothering I don't mean—

Oh, dear Jay, she says, I didn't know. She hugs me hard—she's taller than I am—and when we let go we're both wiping our eyes dumbly and smiling uncomfortable smiles. You should see someone.

Someone?

Have you ever been to a therapist?

No, never.

You should. They help. A little. She hollers through the screen door at her clinical psychologist wife, Right, Hun?

● ● ●

To gather myself, to get some space and some peace, I run the errands that need running, Thisbe's list crushed in my hand, then stuffed into a pocket. I have an awful time getting out of the house, remembering keys, phone, license, ignoring question after question so I might remember to close the damper on the grill, keeping the coals from burning out while I'm gone, and gone I am.

On the way, I find no peace. Also, I lose the list. My entire hourlong trip feels like limitless lifetimes—plural, literal. My sense of time has ballooned, and in that expansion, I encounter redundancies in infinites. By the time I return home, but before Thisbe finds me, I can't climb from the car I've managed to pull into, but not park in, the garage. I am having a full-blown psychotic episode.

My limbic coup d'état has been met with an embarrassing executive retreat and retrenchment. What's left of me—the me I know as my self—has lost the logos of any logic, making all logistics—the organization of movements, the marshaling of limbs—insurmountable. I'm minutely conscious, painstakingly aware, of every cellular sensation necessitating the simplest motion, so much so that each interminable sequence feels overwhelming.

I can't maintain my context long enough to make a first move. But I must try, or I'll die. Because there's something life-threatening I'm not considering. In order to keep from forgetting anything along my never-endian way up and out of the car, I visualize the sequence of events—take foot off brake, leave foot on clutch, yank up parking brake, put car in gear, turn off ignition, pull out keys, pocket keys, take wallet, rolls in bag on passenger seat, vegetables in bin in trunk—and by the time I've reached an end, I've forgotten what I'm supposed to do to begin.

So I sit—in the running car. Exhaust gathers noxiously in the garage. My hands grip the wheel at ten and two, and I'm terrified to take my foot off the clutch, for fear that the front end will lurch through the back wall.

• • •

During this time, the start of the climax of my psychosis, my conscious mind further plummets into the depths of my autonomic systems. I'm currently occupying cognitive locales normally relegated to the sub- and unconscious. Involuntary bodily functions demand voluntary effort and vigilant attention. If I forget my sphincter, my bowels will let loose. If I don't consciously consider breathing, and not simply breathing, and not only each breath, but each individual aspect of every living breath—the tucked pull, up and in, under the heart, to inhale; that peaked, rib-stretching, spine-extending pause; the top-down, pushed exhalation gut-ward; the collapse of the bottom pause that brings about something like a high diver's flip-turn, kicking off the floor of the liver and back up to the surface; only to begin the painstaking cycle over again—then it won't get done, and I'll die. Or so it feels. Especially with all the exhaust I'm inhaling.

• • •

By the time Thisbe finds me, a couple of minutes, by her relative time, after I've pulled into the garage, I've gotten as far as opening the car door. She climbs in the passenger seat, reaches over, and turns off the ignition. She asks, You okay?

• • •

In the throes of my psychosis, I imagine—among sundry delusions—I am dead.

Before my open eyes, I picture a visual flash—back or forward I can't be sure—of me strung up by the neck and swaying—limp, lifeless—from the rope swing I fashioned for Sonne and bound to one of our century-old black walnut trees. I tell her I'm dead. I killed myself.

You're not dead, she says.

I'm not?

No. You didn't kill yourself. She helps me out of the car and into the mother-in-law apartment over our garage. She settles me onto the made guest bed.

During a moment of non sequitur lucidity, I quote from a poem I committed to memory twenty years earlier, a line where Robert Lowell cribs from John Milton offering sympathy for Satan:

> I myself am hell;
> nobody's here—

When less coherent, I confess—falsely but sincerely—to sending surreptitious e-mails to politicians. Absolutely incoherent, I shout seemingly random asides—"Halitosis!"—but in my amped-up mind at the time, nothing is random. Everything is *seeming*; that is, everything is what it is, and also a great deal more than it seems. I am hypersensitive to light, to smell, and to time, my flicker-fusion threshold expanded by adrenaline. I experience a minute the way a mayfly might, and my heart beats like a hummingbird. My vision is telescopic, my hearing bionic. Every single thing—every breath, every mote, every word, every movement and instant—is cause for overawe. I know then—at a cellular level, on a cosmic scale—the nature of God. God is finding fathomless meaning in every single miniscule thing and God—inexhaustible, inexcusable—is terrible.

• • •

For two hours I abide in a spacetime where space dilates, time distends. My stress, and the high-concentration epinephrine coursing through me, permits me to perceive more but process less. Imagine a Sphinx-like creature, a reversed Ganesha, with a human head grafted ridiculously to the body of an elephant. Or, better, hear the narrator of William Blake's "Auguries of Innocence" giving voice to Dr. Seuss's *Horton Hears a Who!* That's more me; I'm part Horton the elephant hearing whole civilizations on specks, part mad Blake envisioning worlds in sand grains, where—or, rather, when—I am infinity, and an hour holds eternity.

Any intelligibility I have in Thisbe's company is short-lived. More often than not, I'm devastated by an inability to form a syllable never mind a full sentence, giving expression to the limitless-in-everything that wings whirling by me. The world is a wheel in a wheel in a wheel in a wheel—the Earth, the solar system, the Milky Way, the universe—and me wheeling along, with all the wheels in wheels within me. I soon suffer another shift and see the wheels aren't simply wheels. Viewed sidelong, they're spirals. At the most intense moments—at this moment—I devolve into crushing inarticulateness, mumbling only, God, God, God, God, God, God, God.

• • •

Thisbe, by and large an atheist, albeit superstitious, said afterward that I sounded like Franny in J. D. Salinger's *Franny and Zooey*, a novel I've never read; this all feels to me like a non-fiction imitation of *The Catcher in the Rye*, the poor man's version, first book to make me weep. I am an old Holden Caulfield gone mad.

Lying on our guest bed, I squeeze shut my eyes, and I see—the horror—a visualization like those vast sand mandalas of the Wheel of Time sprinkle-sculpted by Tibetan monks. Vibrantly colored, cosmically kinetic, the image is a sprawling circum-corpuscular whorl, spiraling, superimposed over the taijitu, the yin-yang symbol. This vision somehow encompasses and embodies a living series of endless dichotomies, all archetypal: dark and light; evil and good; death and life; female and male; straight and gay; night and day; bondage and freedom; sex and love; cosmic and atomic; off and on; on and on . . . The particles in the gyre, each sand grain, are the lives of every life that ever was and ever would be and—this is the worst, most devastating part; the solitude it inspires is absolute—I alone, and for always, am every last one of those innumerable lives and, bafflingly, I am none of them, nothing.

• • •

In each second, I am reborn, live the forever of a lifetime, and die, only to have to survive the infinitude of the next second, and the next. I am certain, at certain moments in the moment, that this is akin to our son's inaugural experience of time, when, as Thisbe and I were acutely aware, there in the neonatal intensive care unit, in those early days of parenting a baby born seven weeks prematurely and housed in an acrylic box—an isolette, they called it—every second felt lifesaving.

• • •

Thisbe, at my bedside in the mother-in-law apartment, keeps telling me, Open your eyes. Her breath is sour.

When I tell Thisbe I am thirsty, she points to the glass of water on the nightstand. When I say I can't lift it, she raises the glass to my lips. When I say I don't know how to drink, having lost all connection to my context, she admonishes me, Of course you do, and I drink.

The thing I keep coming back to, I say, is . . . I'm gay.

You're not gay.

But my first sexual encounters were homosexual.

You were seven. That doesn't count as sexual.

It doesn't? I was seven? You're sure? What if I made it all up?

Now I see, in her sidelong glance, she's looking for an out. Being sucked into my psychosis, where everything gets called into question.

Then I'm gone again—my lucidity, however lunatic, lost to an awful muteness. I experience wave after wave of psychotic panic attacks. Each panic tumbles me through my recurring fears. Returns me round to the refrain of my psychosis: The thing I keep coming back to is . . .

• • •

The thing I keep coming back to is . . . I'm dead. I'm gay. I'm perverted. I must get God. I'm dead . . .

The obvious concern was how to coax me from my psychosis, and Thisbe was unable to do it on her own.

• • •

Tara stands in the bathroom doorway. I've tried to use the bathroom on my own, to piss or shit or both, and I've failed spectacularly. Tara's here to help, or so her librarian smile intimates, if a bit too brightly. She enjoys lending a hand while giving you a ribbing about your dependent predicament. No need to mention your indecent exposure, but I can let you in on a little secret. I think you might've forgotten to pull your pants up. Let's get a closer looksy at your—*ahem*—yes. Just what I feared.

Thisbe's saying this isn't helping, and I don't know if she's talking to me or to Tara down on a knee, making jokes while she and Thisbe resituate my underwear and shorts about my waist.

The thing I keep coming back to, I say, is I'm an alcoholic.

You're not an alcoholic, Thisbe says.

I drink every day.

Jay, you haven't had more than a single beer a night since Sonne was born.

Tara says, Jay, remember at your wedding when Dane, drunk as all hell, streaked through the house naked? Well, now I can say I've seen the penuses of two out of three Nicorvo boys.

Thisbe's laughing, and Tara's laughing, and I'm lying there, inert as a 165-pound sack of testicles.

They get me upright and in between them, a floppy arm

thrown over each of their broad shoulders, and I rally some, held up by them. A helpless man supported by two mothers.

Remember, I say to Tara, when you asked me to be your sperm donor?

I do remember that, Tara says, laughing and rearing back to regard me.

My God, Thisbe says, I forgot about that.

When I said no, I say, you asked me to ask Dane.

Thisbe staggers under her half of my weight. That's right!

Well, Tara says, from what I saw at the wedding, he's got a beautiful keister, that Dane. It obviously runs in the family, and then I'm gone again, mumbling, God, God, God . . .

● ● ●

They walk me like an observant invalid out of the bathroom and onto our screened-in porch, which we call the lanai, depositing me atop the gliding outdoor loveseat. Tara asks how I'm doing.

I holler, Halitosis!

Well, she says, you don't say, breathing into her fist and sniffing. Not me. Can we get you anything? Breath mint?

I say, I have sent . . .

Yes? Tara says.

I've sent—I lower my voice to a whisper—e-mails.

Tara whispers back, Haven't we all.

Thisbe says, What do you mean, e-mails?

To politicians.

You've sent e-mails to politicians?

Isn't that what they're there for, Tara says.

Thisbe says, Why are we all whispering?

Hey, Hon! Tara shouts into the house. I think we could use your professional assistance.

I say, Sexual.

Sexual what? Thisbe says.

Tara says, Healing of course. When Thisbe shakes her head, Tara says, What.

Sexual e-mails, I whisper.

Tara whispers, You mean like sexts?

You've sent sexual e-mails to politicians, Thisbe says.

I nod.

What politicians?

Oh, Hon!

The thing I keep coming back to is . . . I'm gay.

Honey!

And here Laura squats before me, catching my eye, smiling and nodding. Her bedside manner is beautiful. She, too, is tall and lovely, going gray, and, too, by some coincidental trick, she attended college where I grew up. While I was a student, husky and snide, at Sarasota Middle School, Laura was earning her bachelor's degree at New College, just down Tamiami Trail from the Sarasota-Bradenton Airport.

She's got both hands on both of my knees, and she's gently moving her palms, in circular motions, over my kneecaps, saying, If you're gay, Jay, it's okay. She's got a slight Southern accent, a sweet-tea lilt that makes a listener lean in a little nearer. I can't help but want to kiss her. She asks, Because you know what? We're gay, too.

• • •

I'm staring into my lap. On my bare thighs, goose-bumped and wet, rests a stainless steel salad spinner brim-full with ice water. I'm in my underwear. They're boxer briefs.

Tara, having trouble getting my shorts off and over my sneakers, says, Here we are again. Only going the other direction.

I'm resurfacing, but only just, regaining some executive function. The result is abject paranoia. Because these three women—Thisbe, Tara, Laura, all wives, all mothers—are succubae. I am sure of it. They are undoubtedly seducing me.

This is psychosexual assault, not unwelcome. A reconfiguring of my molestation maybe, a ménage à quatre with a couple of lesbians to recast my homosexual child-on-child abuse. Their idea of foreplay is slow psychological torture. They're waterbowling me. Subjecting me to some sort of West Coast kinky dyke meets Polar Bear Club fetish. They are freezing my crotch while depantsing me. My penus has never been so withdrawn, my testicles never this retracted. I will soon be welcomed among the castrati. But first, they must obtain a sperm sample. So here's how lesbians make their babies.

• • •

I'm coming to realize, as I huddle over a frigid salad spinner, how the male-dominated world, as I know it, ends. This unholy trinity of middle-aged ladies are Fates or Furies or a caucus of Muses. They are trying to turn me into a woman. Or get me to admit I'm gay. Possibly force me to confess to some—or to all—sexual deviance. Or persuade me to find a real job. That, or coax me and my damnable soul back to God, who I have no doubt is a butch lesbian. They could be working toward all the above, and all of them ask, in turn, how I'm doing.

The thing I keep coming back to, I say, is I'm dead.

We've already been through this, Laura says.

Then this is after.

After what? Thisbe says.

After life.

Tara says, Aren't *we* heavenly?

What do you mean *we?* I say.

Thisbe can't keep herself from climbing earnestly all aboard my every runaway thought, while Laura provides the grounded clinical guidance, and Tara offers comic relief everyone's in desperate need of, most of all me. But I can't follow the conversation, never mind the asides.

Glenn pops in—all pubescent elbows and knees, gangly as

a harvestman—and he's assigned to keep an eye on Sonne and Ayla, chasing chickens outside and filling glass vials with water from the birdbath. Mikey remains in the woods.

Glenn gives me a long, anxious look—he's a smart kid, and nervous—and I am a man in the convulsions of the matriarchal future he has to look forward to. Then he's gone.

The thing I keep coming back to, I say, is—

It's okay, Jay, Tara says. There's no need.

How do you know?

Because right now, Thisbe says, we know you better than you know you.

I say, Huh?

Laura says, This is a psychotic episode you're having, Jay. It's not real. None of it is. It's all a product of your imagination.

Tara says, Your wild imagination.

Your beautiful imagination, Thisbe says.

Even you?

Laura says, What do you mean?

All three of you.

They laugh and look at each other, shrugging and smiling. Their ease and assurance with each other—a rapport that predates my introduction into their lives and, at present, omits me almost entirely, even though I'm the center of their attentions—says, Yeah, sure, even us, why not.

No, not us, Laura says. We are real. This is real. She splashes a hand in the ice water. What isn't real is all the other stuff. Your insecurities. What's going on inside you. Your head. The scary stories that don't fit in, or fit too well, with this.

This?

All of the things here—she taps my forehead—the things you're thinking. And feeling. Your fears. All that *feels* real, I know, and your feelings are of course very real, but that's not what is happening out here, in the world, with all of us. Those are just your fears, and your trauma, come to the surface. Come back to life.

Trauma, I say. What trauma?

We're real, Thisbe says. Everything else isn't.

You're not dead, Laura says. You haven't sent sexual e-mails to—

Sexts, Tara says.

Not helpful, Laura says. You had a panic attack back in the kitchen. An epic one. It triggered all sorts of stuff. Lord knows what all. And it's wound you into this episode here. But it won't last. I promise. You're safe. We're taking care of you. We love you. Holding my wrists, she dunks my hands into the ice water that overflows onto my thighs. We love you. We all do.

We really do, Thisbe says.

Remember, Tara says, I asked to have your baby.

Thisbe says, And I had your baby.

Cold, I say. Ow.

Laura pulls out my dripping hands gone numb. You're not gay, she says. She dunks my hands back in the salad spinner. Pulls them out. You're not dead.

But I myself am hell, I say. Nobody's here.

You're not hell, Laura says. And we're all here.

Wait, that's from something, Tara says. What's that from?

That is from something, Thisbe says. Oh this'll drive me crazy.

I shout, Halitosis!

Laura says, Let's get him something to hold on to.

Are we losing him? Thisbe says.

Tara says, You mean metaphorically?

No, Honey, I mean actually. We're not losing him. I just need some object, any object.

And why are we doing this? Thisbe asks.

Simple, vivid sensations. Touches. Like cold, like wetness, smoothness, roundness. Certain smells. They can help to jar a person out of psychosis.

Oh my, Thisbe says, this is psychosis?

Depersonalization. Dissociation. Derealization. Yup, this is psychosis.

Tara goes and comes back. How's this?

A tomato, Laura says. Wonderful.

Tara says, Are you being sarcastic?

No, Honey. You did a wonderful job choosing that tomato. I love the tomato you've chosen and I love you for choosing a tomato.

Got it from the CSA box. An heirloom.

I see that, Honey. Now give it here, please.

Tara, refusing to relinquish the tomato, says, Hold the tomato. Get it?

Not helpful, Laura says. Here, Jay, can you do me a favor? Can you hold on to this tomato for me?

I cup my wet hands, achy, over the salad spinner, and Tara fills them with the red ripeness about to burst its skin.

• • •

Sitting on the gliding loveseat next to Thisbe, I must remain still. If I sway us, she gets instantly motion sick.

All the ice is gone from the salad spinner. I'm holding an heirloom tomato with a pulpy split in its deep-pink skin. A brandywine maybe. Its leafy sepal star still attached. The tips of its five points beginning to brown. I recall, vaguely, I'm supposed to give it a sniff from time to time. The fruit doesn't have an odor, but the stem carries a whiff of the tomato plant. Smells like snuff. Like spiced tobacco.

Can I ask a question?

Thisbe says, Always.

Do I still need the salad spinner?

Lifting it, Thisbe sloshes cool water onto my damp lap before setting the steel bowl on the floor.

And why am I holding a tomato in my underwear?

You don't remember?

I do, too well, it's just . . . I think I need to hear you say it.

You can't rock.

I give her a look that must come across part hangdog, part

hound dog. The disappointment of a bad Elvis impersonator whose expression says, *What do you mean I can't rock?* I am *rock.*

The glider, she adds. Don't rock the glider.

Oh. I'm able to grin. I say, You were about to say.

I was about to say you went crazy.

I take a deep breath, say, Just thinking about what all just happened—about what I just put everyone through—what I just did—

You didn't *do* anything.

How *was* I?

The warmth in her eyes is so obvious, the plea in her voice so plaintive, that I'm able to believe, for the time being, I am not presently crazy.

You were you, she says. You but crazy. And sweet. And funny. You told a joke. Which wasn't funny. The funny part was you trying to tell it. Something about losing the car, and then me.

Did I?

Car's in the garage. I'm right here.

When I ask her what else, she says, I was afraid I wasn't going to get you back.

But you did?

Thanks to Laura and Tara, and that tomato, here you are.

I sniff the tomato. I put my hand on Thisbe's hand holding my thigh. If I'm back, I'm not all back, it was all so—

If you get panicky again, do just like Laura said—breathe.

Every time I catch a glimpse of what just went on, I do feel a rush of panic—feels like real awe, like proximity to God, and God's gone crazy. I ask, Where's Sonne?

Eating dinner. With Tara, Laura, and the kids.

Oh shit, the grill!

Taken care of.

But what if I want to start going to church?

I don't know. I think that scares me more than—I think gay I could do. I don't think I could do God.

I'm feeling all panicky again.

Just breathe. Quiet now. Breathe. But don't rock. Try to be in your body. Your body is your temple.

Is it?

I'm kidding. I'm quoting Billy Blanks.

I can't recall who that might be. No kidding right now, I say. I can't take it.

After a time of worked-up quiet, I ask, Will I have to go to a psych hospital? The one in Kalamazoo? Maybe they'll lock me in that padded turret of a water tower. Where they put Malcolm X's mother.

No one's locking you up. Let's just see how you do, okay? Laura says if you have another episode, we should go straight to the ER. But for now, just breathe. Be in your body.

Heart rate high, every muscle taut, overstrained and overstimulated, if my body is a temple, it's in ruins. And my mind, my mind, after its out-of-body interim, doesn't feel like it's mine. The everyday condition of custody, misconstrued, has been overturned. My mind does not belong to me—it's now painfully clear—I belong to my mind. I don't have control; I am controlled. Beholden and hemmed in. A child. Worse, I am an indentured servant to my self. Captive with one chance of freedom: the stark flash of my strung-up body—but not my mind, because my perception hovers some ten feet away and above. There I sway, tongue lolling from my blue and swollen face, dangling over the green, green grass.

This, I will come to learn—after five long years of cognitive behavioral therapy—is suicidal ideation. Thanks in part to my therapy, but mostly due to the love and support I get at home, these thoughts abate, but abatement comes later, and it is hard-fought. It requires forgetting, but only after an enforced, and torturous, period of dark remembrance, where I talk through, and then copy out, all my worst acts and fears as honestly as I'm able.

• • •

My teeth alternate between clenched and clattering. I want to sink my fingers into the tomato. I feel as though I've been dosed with epinephrine after an anaphylactic shock. I'm trembling but not cold. I will never again sleep.

Thisbe asks if I'm okay, and the question—its binary insistence on yes or no, okay or not-okay—makes me frustrated and anxious. Everything is not either A or not-A. Middles exist. Nonbinaries are everywhere. I want her to ask how I am. I want freedom to qualify. Slight difference makes all the difference. I don't want my okayness to be either true or false. Better that it be either true or not-able-to-be-proved-true. I don't know if I'm okay, but my not-knowing is not the same thing as not-being. It's close. But negation isn't failure. Absence of proof is not proof of absence.

I shake my head, want to tell her I'm not feeling okay. But I don't know what I am, never mind what I am feeling. I'm not better; I know that much; I'm finitely worse. I can nearly measure how much.

The strain of maintaining my sanity, now that I have it somewhat back, demands vigilance. I can feel a gravitational draw downward. Bliss is madness. If I lose concentration, I'll relose my mind.

I start forced exhalations. Deep breaths. Each offers assurance, but only some, that I am. I breathe, therefore I am.

That's right, Thisbe says, petting me. Deep breaths.

I am, I say. I add, You're rocking.

It's okay when I rock, she says. I just can't be rocked. Want me to stop?

No. Soothing. And the petting. Don't.

Rock but don't pet?

No, don't stop, rocking or petting.

But I love you so much, she says, and I wait for a qualifier that doesn't follow.

Coming back into myself. Eyes closed. Centering and painstakingly, establishing my context and my syntax, I'm realizing

I've got to reorganize my sanity, if I am to maintain it, starting from zero. I must piece my entire life back together. Reorder it, rewrite it in such a way that, this time, the structure of me isn't so haphazard. I now know how precarious I've been all these years—this, all of this, has been my long overdue collapse. Paradoxically this—all of this—is also the opposite. It is the report of my reconstruction. It's very existence testifies to my want to be a better copy of myself, available, even if I can never be the best.

• • •

There's freedom in letting go. This freedom is terrible. It confirms that chaos lies at the far end of liberty. Physicists call it entropy. Heat death. When all the order leaves a system. I see stretched out before me the psychic wasteland I've just created. My rebuilding will take years, and it begins here, now, by acknowledging my molestation. By acknowledging it, I may keep from repeating it.

The worst is not the molestation. The worst is the secret I am forced to keep, was forced. That secret built a wall—brick by brick, word by word—between my mom and me. Between me and my brothers. Between me and every man, woman, and child I've met, save for the few I've taken into confidence over the years. My molestation and its secret, its shame, is a wall between me and the world. This is me, me pulling down that wall—brick by brick, word by word—and rebuilding something, rebuilding this book, from the salvage.

• • •

Then there's the prevailing feeling I experience in the wake of true existential dread, a feeling somewhat akin to general anxiety but more substantive. A drive. Nearly an internal directive, primed and preprogrammed to launch after a fit of panic. It's more a voice than a bodily sensation. The almost-voice says: *Change your life*.

And change I must. The question is how, and what? The compulsion is met by the confounding possibilities. Go to church. Come out as gay. Hang myself. Find a therapist. Quit writing. Land a real job. Get divorced. Run away.

The dismaying part is this: I love my life with my wife and my son. When I'm here, at home in their company, I am most myself. Of that I'm certain. My wife is not only my favorite person in the world; she's my favorite place. At any given moment, of any given day or night, there is no place I'd rather be than a handsbreadth inside Thisbe Nissen. I don't fantasize about other lives or other lovers. When I fantasize, I fantasize about my wife. I am living out my fantasy, in the present. I don't want a different future. It's my past that poses the problem. It's out in the world, among other people who don't know of my molestation, or when other people come to our home and I have to shut away my molestation, it is then that I am overwhelmed. At home with Thisbe and Sonne, I'm known. They know everything there is to know about me. Home is the place without secrets. That's Godsmark.

As with Thisbe, I keep no secrets from Sonne. Our prime parenting directive has been truth, plain if not simple. I'd recently told him—with as few details as possible—about my molestation at the hands of my babysitter. We figure that when Sonne's ready to ask a question, he's ready to hear a truthful answer. We acknowledge that we are never presenting him with the Truth; we're only ever getting as near to Truth as we can. This—all our openness, fallible but effortful—would be a terrible thing to lose. Maybe the most terrible thing. Yet I feel, down low in my gut, the powerful compulsion to run, to hide.

Thisbe.

Jay.

Could you maybe . . .

She sits up. What do you need, water?

No.

What then?

I don't know, I say, turning silently through my options. Get God. Be gay. Hang myself. Therapy. Quit writing. Find a job. Divorce. Run far, far away.

There is one that throbs among the others. When it occurs to me—ask for help—I feel the most fear, and that's how I know it's most true. That's how I know what to do.

• • •

Sitting there with Thisbe, my lovely and beloved wife, my best friend—ever, and I've had some good ones—I take a breath. I need help, I say. I say, I can't do this alone.

You don't have to.

Tara appears. Laura, too. Maybe they've been listening, that or they never left. When the kids finish eating, Tara says, we're gonna say goodbye.

Laura says, How are you feeling, Jay?

I shake my head. I say, I'm sorry.

There's not one thing to be sorry about. Do you want us to stay?

I think we're okay, Thisbe says, and if not, we'll go straight to the hospital.

• • •

We stand in the driveway waving goodbye. Tara, Laura, and their three kids pile into their rental car. They're spending the night in Grand Rapids before flying home to Portland.

They climb back out of the car to give us one last hug. I apologize anxiously to Glenn; I'm saying I'm sorry to Ayla for not playing with her more; I'm thanking Mikey for the trails he's blazed through our woods. I'm wondering when thoughts of his abuse will begin to intrude, more and more, upon his daily life. Maybe they have. Maybe he is already experiencing what I've just experienced, and always is—a kind of base-line, low-grade disassociation—he's just more open about it. I've shown I share some of his tendencies toward psychosis, and he's been receiving help for years, tended to by therapists, court-appointed counselors, and his librarian and psychologist moms.

I've been dealing with the psychological aftershocks of my childhood sexual abuse for over thirty years, had managed to keep myself in decent working order without so much as a nod in the direction of a mental healthcare professional—less a point of pride than a show of fear—though I'd gravitated in my romantic relationships toward thoroughly therapized partners. Standing beside Thisbe, I realize I've been passively seeking therapy by proxy. This strikes me as selfish, and cowardly, and unfair. This is the first wrong I must right.

• • •

You're dressed now as a barefoot, unmasked Spider Man, having shed your Captain America costume, but you're a Spider Man who plays a mean blues. You, my beloved only son, you blow your harmonica, and hard.

Our guests are all in their rental minivan—Tara and Laura, Glenn, Ayla, and Mikey—buckled in, and you escape our grasp and scramble up and in beside Glenn. Goodbyes take forever, always, and this goodbye is among the longest of my life.

Thisbe retrieves you kicking and laughing, handing you to me. I hold you fast.

You're a happy moppet with a memory that's a little frightening. You have my big brown eyes and Thisbe's wavy brown hair, so full, shaggy, and fun that we can't bring ourselves to have it cut. It bounces to your shoulders, flops over your adorable face.

Holding you in my arms, my forearm under your rear, I feel newly shy, worried I'm touching you in inappropriate ways. I put you down, a failure, as a father, as a man.

As soon as your dirty bare feet touch the ground, you say, Up, Dada, up.

I do as told, relieved that your fears aren't my fears, not yet, and maybe never, not if I can help it.

Wanna hear a song, Dada?

Sure, just gently, I say. You're close to my ear. But we should say goodbye.

You say, This's called "A Sad Song." You blow a few noisy notes, plaintive and drawn out. They do sound sad.

With you at ease in my arms, not crying and whiny now that Tara's fed you a burger—you're a sunny child, if never easy, when you're not hungry—I'm upset and unnerved but less so. Nor am I overwhelmed by your savvy read of my emotional state—a sad song, indeed—and you remind me, daily, how attuned kids are to the adults around them. I sure was when I was your age.

Sonne, Thisbe says, how 'bout not right now, okay? Let's say goodbye. Wave goodbye.

You wave like a fish swims down.

Tara, behind the wheel, opens her window. She says, One, two, three, *Happy birthday, to you* . . .

Laura, Glenn, Mikey, and Ayla join in the serenade. Then Sonne and Thisbe are singing along with.

I'm reminded I'm thirty-nine, halfway along my life's journey, or about to be. I'm blown kisses I feel compelled to catch. I'm rattled but I can't help taking part in the niceties, and they are nice. I'm simply having a hard time believing it all. I don't doubt the sincerity; I doubt reality, but I take part nonetheless. Though it feels a touch false, it still helps, and I've been down enough, and back up again, to know that the feeling of falsity fades. I go through the motions and, eventually, the motions will carry me through to the truth, or some approximation of it.

Another harmonica song, you say.

Sonne, Thisbe says.

Hold on, I say, I have to dry my tears from the last one.

You're smiling, flashing those little milk teeth, knowing I'm kidding, maybe.

Your smile makes me smile—I can't help it—it's a small smile but it's a smile, and it has me feeling a hint of resilience. Your resilience becomes mine. The same way my resilience may, one day, become yours. I did, after all, just make a joke, and a dad joke at that. This says something, doesn't it?

You weave your head back and forth like a blind R&B musician, but you're only trying to get your bangs out of your eyes. You say, Why did you cry?

I'm able to smile a little wider and answer, The song was so sad.

Tara toots the car horn as she K-turns out of the driveway.

How about some exit music, Thisbe says, but gently, please. You are right in Dada's ear.

I'm not in Dada's ear!

No, not in—it's an expression—but you're in his arms very *close* to his ear.

Aren't you hot in that outfit? I ask. All those muscles must be sweltering.

Of course not, you say. What's *sweltering*?

Superhot, Thisbe says.

Next song's called . . . it's called—you begin to gleam as it comes to you, you so obviously please yourself—you say, Next one's called "Song of Unbelievable Lasers," and then you're wailing away, again in my ear.

I lean my head away from the blasts of your loud breath, watching our friends drive down our rural road, Baseline, worrying what comes next for me, for you, for our family, for us all, while you make your music, an impromptu tune with its wild title, a title worth repeating, a title I could never, not in a million tries or lives, have made up on my own, not without you, you and your "Song of Unbelievable Lasers."

Acknowledgments

I want to first acknowledge that on 10 September 2015, a Thursday, I e-mailed a reply to Nelly Reifler, who had the sweet temerity to write and ask, "Jay, how are you?" That's how this memoir, unbeknownst to me, began. As an answer to Nelly's innocent question. Nelly, if you don't bother to check in, this book may not be. I'm afraid I gave you the short answer, then. This is how I am more fully, or how I *was* anyway, back in 2015. Here in 2024—have nine years seriously gone by?—I am doing much better. The very existence of this book, my Exhibit A entered into the record, should testify to that. Sorry it's taken me so long to form a proper response. I should also acknowledge that, given its origins, this book is—in essence— epistolary. It's a love letter, albeit troubled and overlong, to an old friend. It is also a love letter to my young son, Sonne, growing up and into a man, and a good one. Much better than I was at his age, that's for damn sure. This book is a love letter to my wife, Thisbe, who every day makes me feel egregiously lucky and loved. You, Thisbe, are home; you are Godsmark. This book is a love letter to my brothers, Dane and Shawn, to my Aunt Gail, and to all those who helped me get some help, or offered me some support. Like Sterling Watson, a novelist's novelist, and criminally underappreciated, the best stand-in dad a wannabe writer could wish for, who, when he learned a little of what I've narrated here, wrote to tell me exactly what I needed to hear: "I've felt kicked in the gut for a few days now, and wishing that somehow through a time warp I could go back to your past and protect you and of course give that devil what he deserved." If only, Sterl. And so this memoir is, also, a time-warpy love letter to my younger self—or selves. I am here in my future, to say to a surly, husky little scamp, "Don't worry, Jay. It'll be okay." I am also here in what will soon be my past, way back in 2024, telling my older, future self, "Do not give up, you son of a bitch. Not yet. Look what we've done here. There's still more that needs doing." Mostly, though, this memoir is a love letter to my mom, Sharon. Mom, what follows is going to sound a little abstract—and our love, and its expression, couldn't be more tangible, more huggable—but I'm put in mind of the following lines about Samuel Beckett, from Fintan O'Toole's review of *Beckett's Political Imagination* by Emilie Morin: "[Beckett] was left therefore with a paradox: the need to express what he had not experienced, to be witness to what he had not seen. His art would come from having no power to witness, no desire to witness, no authority as a witness—together with the absolute obligation to witness." That, somehow, says it all. Too, it's worth noting that O'Toole, with more clarity and optimism, is echoing Beckett's earlier, darker words: "The expression that there is nothing to express, nothing with which to express, nothing from which to express, no power to express, no desire to express, together with the obligation to express." I better like Fintan's former, even if Samuel's latter got there first. Also, crucially, some ten years ago, I placed a cold call to the office of the Fort Monmouth site manager in New Jersey, asking to get my hands on an old criminal investigation report, if such a thing existed. A day later, Lieutenant Colonel John E. Occhipinti left me a voicemail. I still have that message. I just listened to it, for what must've been the fiftieth time. I queue it up when I falter, and I queue it up when I don't. The warm Jersey-boy baritone of LTC Occhipinti, who would want me to call him John, is so soothing, so reassuring and commanding, that it has continuously lent me the confidence to soldier on.

John's steady expression sounds to me like the best of home, and if he doesn't return my call that day, doesn't leave me with that encouraging recording, I would've given up before I got started. And now I feel compelled to acknowledge how much I've changed, and how often, in the writing of this book, and in the living of this life. I'm sorry, but I do not understand people who say people don't, or can't, change. That is just the dumbest shit. I have known so much change that I have difficulty reconciling my myriad versions. All the innumerable mes. Copies upon copies, changing all the while, in an ever-changing world. And who's to say which is best? Not me, not with any real authority. So here's to all of you who've seen me through some of my changes, to those of you who can acknowledge having changed right along with me, and to all of you who've aided and abetted this misdemeanor of a memoir as it has changed from bad to better. Without you, this copy here would be mediocre, at best, and it would also be wholly unavailable. Topmost among the folks who ushered this finished book into the world is Geoff Dyer. Geoff picked my manuscript out of a lot, and I am almost certain he did so with a hand covering his eyes, intoning, in an especially adorable English accent, "Eeny, Meeny, Miny, Moe." Thank you, Geoff. I do need to acknowledge the debts I owe to the very good Dawgs at the University of Georgia Press, particularly Beth Snead, who is an organizational marvel; Elizabeth Adams; Christina Cotter; Lea Johnson; Steven Wallace; Kaelin Chappell Broaddus; and Jason Bennett. Ivo Fravashi's masterful copyedits have made me less confusing, even to myself—and she tried her hardest to temper my overuse of the em dash. Nicole Dewey has been more than a great advocate; she's been a phenomenal friend: smart, savvy, and kind as can be. She's got the hospitality of a born Southerner but the sharp elbows of a lifelong New Yorker. Those two seemingly contrary qualities make for an ideal book publicist. Hard to imagine we go back almost twenty years, Nicole, and it doesn't hurt that you bake a mean challah and that you spent your childhood summers in Sarasota—where I like to think we crossed paths, unknowingly, on Siesta Key, in our bathing suits. Jennifer Carlson believed in this book long before it was a book, when it was merely a bunch of pages of crazy. See, Jenster, you were right all along. I give a rousing round of applause to Phosphorescent, aka Matthew Houck, for letting me borrow a few lines from one of his incantatory songs. I owe a debt to Kevin Larimer at *Poets & Writers*, who published an essay, "The Unwilling Suspension of Disbelief," wherein I first acknowledged my sexual abuse in nonfiction. If not for Kevin's care with that essay, and me, I'm not sure I take a stab at this memoir. I am obliged to Sue William Silverman for helping make possible the AWP award for creative nonfiction, and to everyone at the Association of Writers and Writing Programs, especially James Tate Hill, who got to be the bearer of the good news. JT, I am sorry I thought your congratulatory e-mail was a sophisticated—and wonderfully written—phishing scam. I must here acknowledge that you were not out to steal my money, my identity, or my memoir. In fact, you and AWP bestowed upon me these very things. I'm indebted to Susan Weaver, who helped me to know how important it is to talk with someone about all this stuff, and more. Talk is no simple task for a writer like me, who believes words have real value, and are a limited resource worth saving for when they are most needed. So quit your reading already and go find someone to talk to, for fuck sake, but don't expect it to help. Not at first. At first, it hurts, and not like hell. The hurt is the hell. A hell that distorts and disorients. And it is a hell not of your own making— that is the most vicious part—even if it is the worst possible hell you can imagine. You've got to talk your way on out, and maybe even write your way through, like the middle-aged Medieval Italian poet-in-exile once did. In so doing, I got zero catharsis. At first, for me, it even did more harm than good, the writing more harmful than the talking. But then, eventually, it does get better. A little, and little by little. Because I never did feel the lifting of a great weight. What I felt, ultimately, was the daily presence of that weight—here it is now—one I had to hoist every Goddamn morning, in order to get stronger, in order to get better. Talk of abuse is work, good work but hard work. The more you work at it, the easier it does get. But it never gets easy. And be careful. Because you can overdo it. Too much talk, I find, can be every bit as bad as no talk at all. RAINN (Rape, Abuse and Incest National Network) is, in my limited opinion, the best anti-sexual violence organization in the nation. Check them out. They operate a hotline (call 800.656.HOPE, or you can chat online at www.rainn.org) in partnership with local service providers across the country. Working your stuff out can put terrible strain on your loved ones. It helps, both them and you, to have someone else to go to, but someone—preferably a professional—who knows what in hell they're doing. Lastly, I feel a responsibility to call attention to the kid who molested me as a kid. Don't worry, I will not out you, not here, of all places. You know who you are. That's enough, for now. And I am sorry but I cannot forgive you, can never forgive you, I'm afraid. But I can, finally, acknowledge what you've done. Can you?

About the Author

Jay Baron Nicorvo's memoir, *Best Copy Available*, won the AWP Award judged by Geoff Dyer. He's published a novel, *The Standard Grand*, and a poetry collection, *Deadbeat*. His nonfiction has twice been named "Notable" in *Best American Essays*. Jay has served as an editor at PEN America, the literary magazine of the PEN American Center, and at *Ploughshares*. He spent years as membership director of the Community of Literary Magazines and Presses in NYC. A proud community college graduate, he's taught at Eckerd College, Cornell College, Emerson College, and Western Michigan University. He lives with his wife, Thisbe Nissen, their son, a couple of cats, a dog, and a dozen chickens on a defunct farm outside of Battle Creek, Michigan. Find Jay at www.nicorvo.net.

A NOTE ON THE TEXT

The text of this book was set by Kaelin Chappell Broaddus in
Joanna Nova Book, a font in the Joanna family of typefaces designed by Eric Gill (1882–1940), the noted English stonecut-
ter, typographer, illustrator, and sex offender. Named for his
youngest daughter and inspired by Renaissance calligraphy,
Joanna forgoes frills. The spare, sharp, and squared serifs give
the type a modernist bent. Gill set his best-known book, *An
Essay on Typography*, long considered his masterpiece, in Joanna,
which he called *a book face free from all fancy business.* A friend of
Gill's, the British editor and novelist Robert Harling, described
Joanna as groundbreaking: *the letter-forms have character and beauty,
discipline and gaiety. No other alphabet of this century has managed
to make typographical affectation so readable . . . defiant of almost every typographical canon of the day . . . Joanna Italic is gaily triumphant.*
Notable uses of Joanna have included the Penguin Modern
Classics—before the series switched to Helvetica—and Joanna
is the corporate typeface of the United States Department of
Homeland Security. A champion of small-press publishing, Gill
is listed in the *Oxford Dictionary of National Biography* as the *greatest
artist-craftsman of the twentieth century: a letter-cutter and type designer
of genius.* Gill, a Catholic convert, has fallen from some cultural
grace, decades after the revelations divulged in his diaries: his
lifelong sexual relationship with his sister Gladys, the rape of
his eldest daughters—Betty and Petra, but not Joanna—and,
very probably, the family dog.